MODELING AND DESIGNING ACCOUNTING SYSTEMS

Using Access to Build a Database
Second Edition

C. JANIE CHANG, PH.D.

San Jose State University

LAURA R. INGRAHAM, PH.D.

San Jose State University

JOHN WILEY & SONS, INC.

We dedicate this book to our families:
Dan and Casey
Ted, Theresa, and Brenda
We are eternally grateful to them for their constant love and support.

To order books or for customer service please, call 1-800-CALL WILEY (225-5945).

Printed in the United States of America.

ISBN 978-1-119-94709-7

Printed and bound by EPAC.

10 9 8 7 6 5 4 3 2 1

TO THE STUDENT

Accounting information systems have evolved from general ledger packages to database management systems. In fact, for larger organizations, accounting information systems are part of a larger enterprise information system, which by definition, is a database management system. These systems provide accountants and management with the requisite information needed to make the important day-to-day decisions, to control operations, and to make strategic plans for the future.

The traditional database design methodology approach is the normalization approach. However, there is another methodology approach, based upon semantic data modeling, which was created specifically for the design of accounting information systems, known as the REA data modeling approach. This REA approach is the conceptual model methodology that we follow in this text. Although it is hardware and software-independent, we will utilize *Microsoft Access 2010* to implement the data models we create throughout this text.

This book provides you with the concepts underlying data modeling theory, as well as practice in applying these concepts and implementing those concepts in a database design. You begin with the concepts of data modeling in Chapters 1 and 2. The application of these concepts to database design using *Access* is introduced in Chapter 3.

You will begin to build an accounting information system in Chapters 4 through 6. The Sales/Collection Business Process in Chapter 4 allows you to develop your skills in building tables, forms, simple queries, and a basic report. The Acquisition/Payment Business Process in Chapter 5 explores complex queries, forms, and reports. You will create more complex queries, as well as simple macros, and imbed internal macros in table designs in the Human Resource Business Process in Chapter 6.

As you work through the step-by-step instructions in these chapters, you will gain the experience of building an accounting information system. In addition, we have provided multiple choice and discussion questions for you, as well as additional problems that build upon the preceding work, at the end of each chapter to enhance your learning.

TO THE INSTRUCTOR

Accounting information systems has proven to be one of the more challenging concepts to teach in the curriculum. There are several reasons for this. One is that there is no agreement as to how many courses are ideal in terms of coverage of the topic. Many schools offer a single course, others have two courses, and very few others offer a full major in the area of accounting information systems.

This book is intended to be a supplement to any text that is utilized in either an introductory AIS course or a database modeling and design course. It provides you with both a conceptual and a practical approach to data modeling for a resource-event-agent (REA) perspective and database design using *Microsoft Access 2010* as a platform. The first two chapters provide the fundamental concepts and theory for data modeling. Later chapters provided step-by-step detailed instructions for students to follow as they begin to model and design three essential processes of accounting information systems. Chapter 3 provides the essential instructions for students as they begin to explore the basics of *Microsoft Access*. They are exposed to the creation of tables, as well as two very basic forms. In Chapter 4 through 6, students explore the sales/collection process, the acquisition/payment process and the human resources/payroll process, respectively, with a partial database that has already been created for them. Here they have the opportunity to build more complex forms. In addition, they begin building simple queries and quickly move to more advance queries.

In this edition, we have expanded the end-of-chapter multiple-choice questions, discussion questions, and additional problems for students to further challenge the students once they have completed the chapter exercises. We have also added an examination of the SQL (Structured Query Language) that underlies the queries they create.

ABOUT THE AUTHORS

C. Janie Chang is the Vern Odmark Professor of Accountancy at San Diego State University (SDSU). She received her Ph.D. from the University of California, Irvine. Before coming to SDSU, Dr. Chang served as Professor of Accounting Information Systems (AIS) at San Jose State University (SJSU) and at California State University San Marcos. During her time at SJSU, she developed the undergraduate AIS program and founded the SJSU student chapter of ISACA. At SDSU, she established the AIS track in the Master of Science in Accountancy Program. Dr. Chang's teaching interests include AIS related topics (e.g., AIS Development, AIS Audit and Control, Data Modeling/Database Management, Issues in E-business, and Business Networks and Controls) and financial/managerial accounting. Since 2001, she has been an Academic Advocate for ISACA to promote education and career in information systems audit. From 2009 to 2011, she chaired the Education Committee of the Strategic and Emerging Technologies Section of the American Accounting Association. Dr. Chang has studied issues in auditing, accounting, and information systems to investigate professional judgments and decisions in auditing and managerial accounting. Her studies have been published in *Abacus, Auditing: A Journal of Practice and Theory, Behavioral Research in Accounting, Data Base, the International Journal of Accounting, Journal of Accounting Literature, Journal of Multinational Financial Management*, etc. Currently, Dr. Chang is the co-editor of the *Review of Accounting and Finance*, and the editor-in-chief of the *Journal of Contemporary Accounting*.

Laura R. Ingraham is a Professor of Accounting Information Systems at San Jose State University (SJSU). She received her Ph.D. from Arizona State University. Before coming to SJSU, Dr. Ingraham was on the faculty at North Carolina State University and at California State University San Marcos. Dr. Ingraham teaches a broad spectrum of accounting information systems courses at both the masters and undergraduate levels including Accounting Information Systems, Advanced Accounting and Information Systems, Accounting Topics in IT Audit, Systems Development in AIS, Issues in E-Business and Advanced Accounting Information Systems. Dr. Ingraham has also developed a course in Forensics in an AIS Security Framework. As well as strengthening these pedagogical areas, Dr. Ingraham brings years of professional experience in the areas of both taxation and audit to her teaching portfolio. Dr. Ingraham has been the faculty advisor for the SJSU-ISACA student group since 2003 and serves as an Academic Advocate for ISACA, working as a liaison between ISACA and the students to promote both their education and their careers in information systems audit. Dr. Ingraham chaired the Western Region Strategic & Emerging Technologies (SET) Section of the American Accounting Association (AAA) from 2007 to 2008 and has been a member of the CPE Committee of the SET Section since 2009. In addition, she was the Southeast Regional Co-Director of the Teaching & Curriculum Section for the AAA from

2000 to 2002. Dr. Ingraham's research interests incudes issues in accounting information systems, privacy and security, education, taxation, and business process maturity. Her studies have been published in *Accounting: Organizations and Society, Journal of Australian Taxation, Journal of State Taxation, Strategic Finance, The New Review of Applied Expert Systems and Emerging Technologies,* and *The CPA Journal.*

ACKNOWLEDGMENTS

The authors would like to express their gratitude to their publishing team at John Wiley & Sons, Inc., specifically, Chris DeJohn, Sarah Vernon, and Brian Kamins, for their continuing support and belief in this book. In addition, we would like to express our belated gratitude to Donoghue Clarke, without whose editorial efforts the first edition of this book would never have come to fruition, and to Megan Bermudez for her editorial efforts on the second edition.

TRADEMARKS

Microsoft and Access are registered trademarks. Screen shots are reprinted by permission from Microsoft Corporation.

TABLE OF CONTENTS

CHAPTER 1

BUSINESS PROCESSES, DATA MODELING AND INFORMATION SYSTEMS

INTRODUCTION

Despite the rapid growth in networks and information technology, many companies today are still using separate subsystems in their daily operations to support such specialized functions as marketing information systems, accounting information systems, personnel information systems, etc. When management professionals make decisions based on information obtained within one functional area, those decisions, which are apt to be made from a narrow perspective, may not be in the best interest of the company. Given the current business environment, companies should carefully examine every step in their business processes and question the necessity of each step. It is critical for companies to use the power of modern information technology, such as enterprise resource planning (ERP) applications, to improve company performance.

The database approach emphasizes the integration and sharing of data across major functional areas based on the company's business processes. This approach requires a fundamental reorientation or shift in business processes, starting with top management and affecting all employees. That is, the design of an information system is event-driven according to business processes. The purpose of this chapter is to start from the top and use data models to describe a company's business processes. Later chapters will use this business-process-based data modeling approach to assist you in learning how to design a relational database for the company. After completing this chapter, you should be able to:

- Identify resources, events, and agents (REA) in a data model
- Develop basic data models
- Recognize and evaluate the cardinalities in a data model
- Model a company's business processes using an REA diagram

BUSINESS PROCESSES AND DATA MODELING

Data modeling is the process of creating a logical representation of the structure of a database based on a company's business processes. This is the most important task in the development of an effective database that can provide useful information for decision making. A commonly used business data modeling technique is called the Entity-Relationship Diagram (ERD). The ERD uses a graphical representation to identify and document various entities and the relationships between those entities. Three major components of an ERD are entities, relationships, and attributes. An entity is anything about which a company would like to

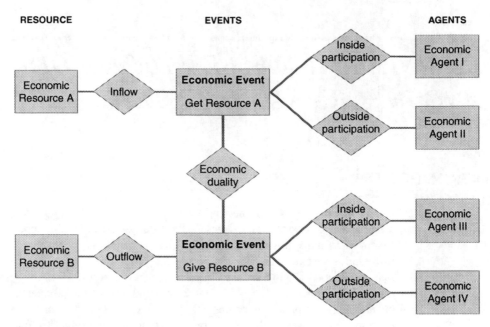

FIGURE 1-1 The REA Pattern
Adapted from McCarthy (1982).

collect and store information, such as "inventory," "purchase," and "vendor." A relationship is an association between entities, such as one or many inventory items included in each purchase transaction. An attribute is a characteristic of an entity, such as the inventory number and the description of each item in the entity of "inventory."[1] In an ERD, rectangles are used to indicate entities, diamonds are used to represent relationships between entities, and small circles are used to show the attributes of each entity. Using an ERD makes it relatively easy to understand a company's business processes and the relationships for those involved entities. The ERD promotes communications between domain experts (such as accountants) and information technology (IT) professionals.

Based on the Entity-Relationship technique, the Resource-Event-Agent model (REA) is a framework specifically designed for building accounting information systems in a shared data environment.[2] First conceptualized by William E. McCarthy in 1982, it captures business processes by categorizing entities into economic resources, economic events, and economic agents. *Resources* are those things that have economic value to a company, such as cash and inventory. *Events* are the various business processes conducted in a company's daily operations, such as sales and purchases. *Agents* are the people and/or organizations that participate in business events, such as customers and salespeople. Adapted from McCarthy (1982), Figure 1-1 shows the most basic REA pattern for modeling business processes. A general rule for creating REA diagrams is that each economic event should be linked to at least one economic resource and two economic agents (one internal and one external to the organization).

[1]The concepts about attributes will be discussed in detail in the next chapter.
[2]McCarthy, W. E. 1982. The REA accounting model: A generalized framework for accounting systems in a shared data environment. *The Accounting Review* (July): 554–578.

The relationship shown between the two economic events in Figure 1-1 (Get Resource A and Give Resource B) is referred to as an economic duality relationship. This is the causal relationship that occurs as a result of a give event (an economic decrement or an outflow) and a take event (an economic increment or an inflow). For example, in a revenue cycle, the give event is most likely the sales event (an outflow of inventory) and the take event is typically the cash receipts event (an inflow of cash). In an expenditure cycle, the give event is usually the cash disbursements event (an outflow of cash) and the take event is typically the purchases event (an inflow of inventory).

REA MODELS AND TRANSACTION CYCLES

The database development process begins with enterprise modeling to set the range and general contents of organizational databases. This can be done effectively and efficiently by organizing an organization's subsystems around certain types of repetitive transactions. These groups of related transactions are called transaction cycles. Although different companies have different transactions, most companies have some transaction cycles in common: revenue, expenditure, human resource/payroll, and financing cycle. For manufacturing companies, the conversion/production cycle is another important component of their information systems.

Figure 1-2 shows the most basic economic events in the five transaction cycles. The revenue cycle includes the sale and cash receipt events. The expenditure cycle includes the

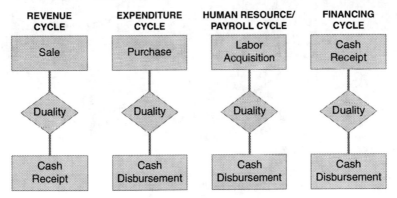

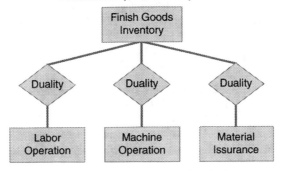

FIGURE 1-2   Basic Economic Events in Transaction Cycles

purchase and cash disbursement events. In addition, a company must acquire labor and pay wages/salaries through the human resources/payroll cycle. The financing cycle includes the events of obtaining funds from investors and/or creditors and paying them back. The conversion/production cycle involves the utilization of labor and machinery to transform materials into finished goods.

The transaction cycles in Figure 1-2 are combined in Figure 1-3 to create an REA model of the entire accounting information system. This high-level conceptual model indicates how the transaction cycles interact with each other and with the financial reporting system.

Figure 1-4 provides sample REA diagrams for each of the transaction cycles. Focusing on the expenditure cycle, a purchase transaction is made between a purchasing

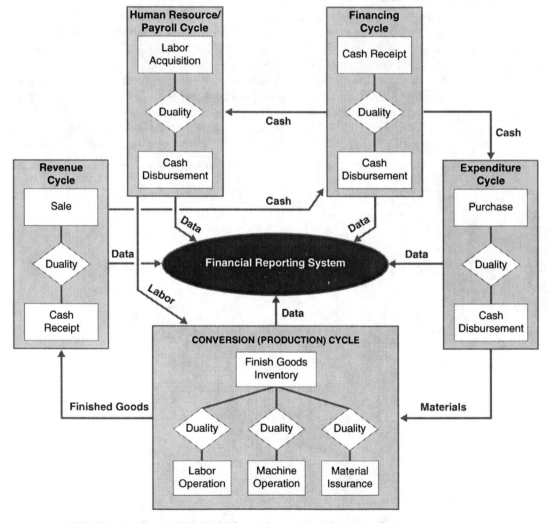

FIGURE 1-3 Overall REA Model for an Accounting Information System

Adapted from Romney, M. B. and P. J. Steinbart. 2012. *Accounting Information Systems.* 12th ed. Englewood Cliffs, New Jersey: Prentice Hall. (page 7)

agent and a vendor and will increase inventory stocks. The purchase transaction will be paid by using cash and involves the vendor and cashier in a cash disbursement event. In the revenue cycle, each sale transaction will decrease inventory, and a salesperson and a customer will participate in the transaction. The sales transaction will be paid by receiving cash involving the participation of the customer and the cashier in a cash receipt event. Note that, as we design the system that models these transactions, each entity needs to be shown only once. That is, there is just one "vendor" entity and one "customer" entity shown on Figure 1-4 despite the fact that the company has many vendors and customers.

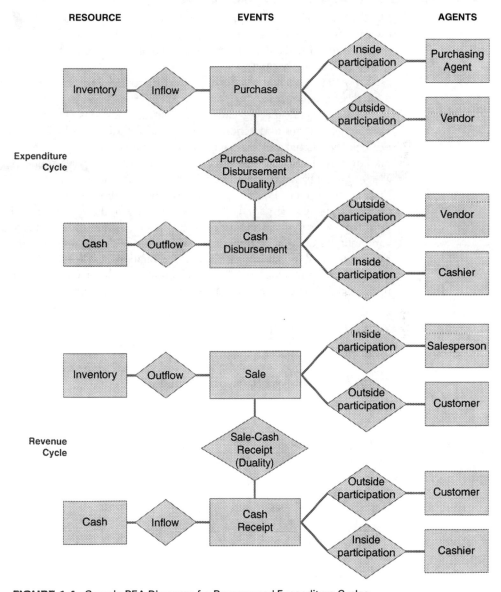

FIGURE 1-4 Sample REA Diagrams for Revenue and Expenditure Cycles

Please notice that a short diagonal line in the lower right-hand corner of one entity (such as Vendor) shows that this entity has been previously shown in another place in the diagram. This is not only to remind the reader that each specific entity will be a table in a database and the database should not have duplicated tables representing the same entity but also to tell the programmer that he or she will find this table and its attribute in another place in the diagram.

CARDINALITIES OF RELATIONSHIPS

Identification of relationships is a very important step in data modeling. A relationship establishes a logical connection between entities. Relationship examples in generic settings include (1) Eric majors in finance; (2) Ben owns vehicle#104; and (3) Professor John Lewis teaches marketing (see Figure 1-5).

For data modeling purposes, Figure 1-6 provides corresponding diagrams to describe these three relationships.

Note that identifying entities and adding relationships to the diagrams are still insufficient in terms of describing how an entity participates in a specific relationship. For example, we should indicate that each student may major in one or more fields. One person may own zero vehicles, one vehicle, or many vehicles. The number of instances of one entity that can be linked to one specific instance of another entity is defined as a *cardinality*. With the information that the cardinalities provide at both ends of each relationship, we can easily understand the participation of each entity in the relationship. That is, cardinality information restricts the number of participation constraints in a relationship. In this book, cardinality is denoted as (*min, max*) where *min* is the minimum number and *max* is the maximum number that can participate in a relationship. What is the correct set of cardinalities in each relationship? Does each entity have a fixed set of cardinalities for all the relationships? The answer depends on the problem domain that you need to model.

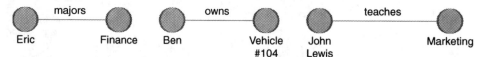

FIGURE 1-5 Sample Relationship Representation

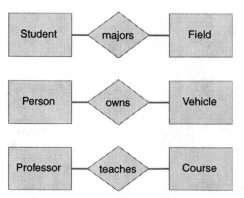

FIGURE 1-6 Sample ER Models

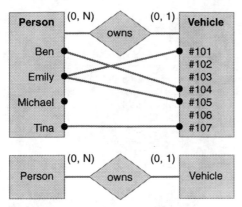

FIGURE 1-7 Person-Vehicle Example

Regarding the person-vehicle example above, assume that Ben, Emily, and Tina own vehicle#104, vehicle#101 and vehicle#105, and vehicle#107, respectively. In addition, Michael does not own any vehicles. We can use the graphical representation in Figure 1-7 to show the relationship and cardinalities.

In Figure 1-7, Emily owns two vehicles. Michael does not own any vehicle. Each of the other two people owns one vehicle. Thus, the cardinalities in this specific "person owns vehicle" relationship is (0, N) near the person entity, which means each person can own at least zero vehicles and at most many vehicles. "N" here means many. The cardinalities of (0, 1) near the vehicle entity indicate that each vehicle may not be owned by a person yet, but each vehicle can be owned by at most only one person.[3]

Another example is the professor-course relationship. Figure 1-8 indicates that each professor teaches at least one course and may teach many courses. Furthermore, different

	Notation for each cardinality	Diagram format to the person-vehicle example
Chen (used in this textbook)	Min zero = (0, Min one = (1, Max one = , 1) Max many = , N)	Person (0, N) owns (0, 1) Vehicle
Crow's Foot	Min zero = ⊖ Min one = ┼ Max one = ┤ Max many = ⤜	Person ├○ ○⤜ Vehicle
HDC	Min zero = (0, Min one = (1, Max one = , 1) Max many = , *)	Person (0, 1) (0, *) Vehicle

[3]This book uses Chen's notation for cardinalities. There are other commonly used notations: Crow's Foot and HDC. The following comparison is adapted from Dunn, C. L., J. W. Cherrington and A. S. Hollander, 2005, *Enterprise Information Systems*, New York: McGraw-Hill. (page 59)

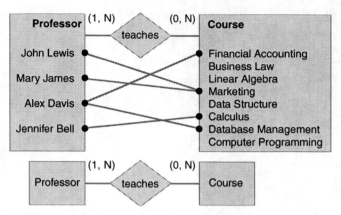

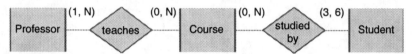

FIGURE 1-8 Professor-Course Example

FIGURE 1-9 Professor-Course-Student Example

professors can teach the same course in different sessions. Finally, not all courses are taught every semester, i.e., some courses may not be offered in a particular semester (some might be Fall semester courses, others might be Spring semester courses). In this example, professors John Lewis and Mary James both teach the marketing course, and no one is teaching business law in the current semester. For this type of relationship, we employ (1, N) near the "Professor" entity to represent that each professor teaches at least one and at most many courses. We employ (0, N) near the "Course" entity to show that each course can be taught by at least zero or at most many professors.

We may also add another entity called "Student," as well as its relationship, "Course is studied by Student," to the diagram (see Figure 1-9). For this example, we will assume all students are full-time. We want to impose the restriction that each student must take at least 3 courses but no more than 6 courses in a semester. In addition, each course can be taken by at least zero or at most many students, same as a relationship between the entities of professor and course. Accordingly, the cardinalities (0, N) and (3, 6) are added to the diagram.

USING REA TO MODEL BUSINESS PROCESSES

There are three basic steps to construct an REA diagram to depict a company's business processes. After the business processes are modeled, the REA diagram should be validated by the company's experts who are knowledgeable about the details and objectives of the business processes. The three steps in developing an REA diagram are as follows:

1. Identify economic exchange events.
2. Identify the resources affected by each economic event and the agents who participate in those events.
3. Determine the cardinalities of each relationship.

The following section provides an example that demonstrates how to use the REA to model a small company's business processes.

Cherokee Art and Antique Store

Background   The Cherokee Art and Antique Store sells original art and antique pieces. Its owner, Jesse Lewis, started the store in 1990 in a small town with a rich Native American culture. Jesse carries original paintings, crafts, jewelry and special antiques from local Native American artists and antique sellers. Since he carries only original pieces of art and craft and antiques, no two items are the same. He displays all available art and antique pieces in the store. Jesse has no employees to help him, so he takes care of all the selecting, buying, and selling himself.

Cherokee's Revenue Cycle   All sales occur in the store. Sales to customers consist of one or more pieces of art and/or the antiques displayed in the store. Jesse accepts cash, checks, and credit or debit cards for sales. However, he requires that all customers pay in full for each transaction. He also requires that each invoice be paid for separately. Jesse goes to the bank every day to deposit daily cash receipts. Although Jesse has a couple of bank accounts for the Cherokee Art and Antique Store, he always deposits his daily revenue into the general checking account.

Model the Revenue Cycle Using REA   **To model business processes in the revenue cycle for the Cherokee Art and Antique Store (Cherokee), we first need to identify economic exchange events in the cycle.** Recall that in Figure 1-2 there are two basic events for any revenue cycle: "Sales" and "Cash Receipt." According to the descriptions stated in the previous paragraph, we can determine that these two events are proper for Cherokee. Therefore, the partial REA diagram in Figure 1-10 can be drawn.
    The second step is to identify the resources affected by each economic event and the agents who participate in those events. For the "Sales" event, inventories of art and antiques are reduced and the participating agents are a customer and Jesse. For the "Cash Receipt" event, Jesse receives payment from the customer. Accordingly, the REA in Figure 1-11 provides the basic business model for Cherokee's revenue cycle.

FIGURE 1-10 *Sales-Cash Receipt Relationship*

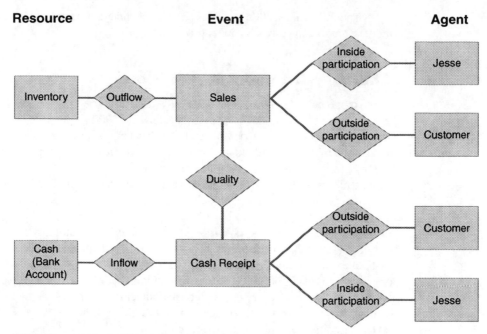

FIGURE 1-11 Basic REA Diagram for Cherokee's Revenue Cycle

The next step is to determine the cardinalities for each event in each relationship. First, notice in Figure 1-12 that "Bank Account" is added to the resource "Cash," because this describes where the inflow of cash is recorded. According to the description of Cherokee's cash collection processes, the relationship between "Bank Account" and "Cash Receipt" should be (1, N) and (1, 1). In other words, a bank account will have at least one cash receipt deposit but can have many deposits. Each cash receipt is deposited into one, and only one, bank account.

Figure 1-13 indicates that the relationship between "Inventory" and "Sales" is (0, 1) and (1, N). Each art piece or antique may not be sold yet; if it is sold, it can be sold only once, since each item is original and unique. Hence, the minimum cardinality is zero and maximum cardinality is one for the "Inventory" entity. For each sale transaction, at least one piece of inventory and, at most, many pieces of inventory can be sold. Therefore, for the "Sales" entity, the minimum cardinality is one, and the maximum cardinality is many.

FIGURE 1-12 Cash-Cash Recipt Relationship

FIGURE 1-13 Inventory-Sales Relationship

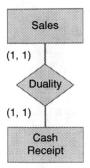

FIGURE 1-14 Sales-Cash Receipt Relationship

In Figure 1-14, we see that the relationship between "Sales" and "Cash Receipt" is (1, 1) and (1, 1). Each sale transaction has one, and only one, cash receipt, and each cash receipt event is for one sale transaction only. Recall that, in the description above, all customers must pay in full at the time when the transaction occurs and that each invoice is paid for separately. In other words, there are no accounts receivable, no partial payments, and no combined payments. Therefore, the cardinalities are (1, 1) on the "Sales" side. In addition, on the "Cash Receipt" side, the cardinalities are also (1, 1).

If Cherokee bills customers periodically (for a few transactions), then the cardinalities would be (1, N) on the "Cash Receipt" side as indicated in Figure 1-15. In that case, each cash receipt would be related to many sales transactions (allowing for combined payments). Due to the fact that customers could delay payments (i.e., monthly billing), Cherokee would have accounts receivables. This would result in a scenario of **accounts receivable** as indicated by the **zero** minimum cardinality at the "Sales" side. If customers still must pay in full, the maximum cardinality at the "Sales" side is one.

Figure 1-16 provides the complete REA diagram for Cherokee's revenue cycle. In terms of the cardinalities between events and agents, the general case is (1, 1) on the event side and (1, N) on the agent side. Each sale transaction relates to one customer only, and each customer can participate in many sale transactions. Here, the internal agent, Jesse, is denoted in a dotted-line box that means he is the only person conducting the sale transactions; thus, we do *not* need to track information about him. In addition, in the REA diagram, we need to illustrate each entity once only. Therefore, we do not need to show two rectangles for the "Customer" entity and "Jesse."

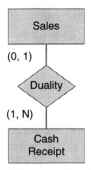

FIGURE 1-15 Sales-Cash Receipt Relationship (with Accounts Receivable)

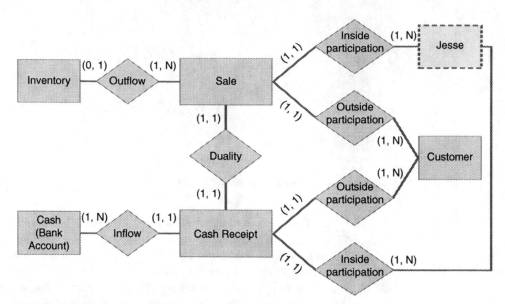

FIGURE 1-16 Complete REA Diagram for Cherokee's Revenue Cycle

Cherokee's Expenditure Cycle Sometimes, Jesse does not pay the artist or seller of art and antique pieces when the pieces are delivered by the artists/sellers. Most of the artists and sellers know him very well and are willing to let Jesse pay them later. In addition, since each purchase may include multiple items, most artists are willing to let Jesse pay them in installments. Jesse always writes a check to pay each artist or seller (i.e., he never pays using a credit card) and he sometimes pays for items on several different invoices at one time.

Model the Expenditure Cycle Using REA To model business processes in the *expenditure* cycle for Cherokee, we first identify economic exchange events in the cycle. Recall that in Figure 1-2 there are two basic events for any expenditure cycle: "Purchase" and "Cash Disbursement." According to the descriptions stated in the previous paragraph, we can see that these two events are proper for Cherokee. Therefore, the partial REA diagram in Figure 1-17 can be drawn.

The second step is to identify the resources affected by each economic event and the agents who participate in those events. For the "Purchase" event, inventories of art and antique are purchased, and the participating agents are the artist/seller and Jesse. For the "Cash Disbursement" event, Jesse can pay each artist/seller in cash installments. The REA diagram in Figure 1-18 shows the basic business model for Cherokee's expenditure cycle.

The next step is to determine the cardinalities for each event in each relationship. Since Cherokee's checks are written from one account only and at least one and at most many checks can be written from the bank account, the relationship between "Bank Account" and "Cash Disbursement" should be (1, N) and (1, 1) as indicated in Figure 1-19.

Figure 1-20 shows us that the relationship between "Inventory" and "Purchase" is (1, 1) and (1, N). That is, each art and antique piece can be purchased only once, as every item is

FIGURE 1-17 Purchase-Cash Disbursement Relationship

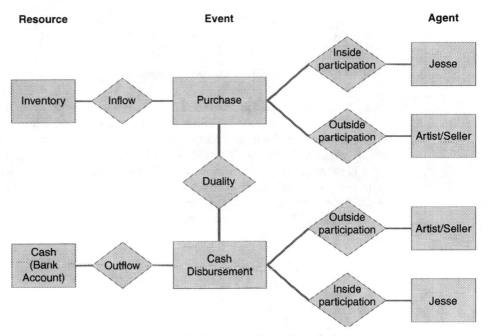

FIGURE 1-18 Basic REA Diagram for Cherokee's Expenditure Cycle

FIGURE 1-19 Cash-Cash Disbursement Relationship

unique and original. For each purchase transaction, at least one piece of inventory and at most many pieces of inventory can be acquired.

The relationship between "Purchase" and "Cash Disbursement" is (0, N) and (1, N) as shown in Figure 1-21. In other words, Jesse might not pay for the items at the time of purchase. This is the zero at the "Purchase" side which shows that there are accounts payable.

FIGURE 1-20 Inventory-Purchase Relationship

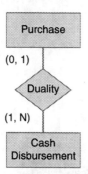

FIGURE 1-21 Purchase-Cash Disbursement Relationship

Each purchase maybe paid in installments, so the maximum cardinality at the "Purchase" side is many (N). In addition, each cash disbursement (i.e., a check) is at least for one purchase or at most for many purchases, since Jesse may pay for items on several different invoices from an artist at one time. The cardinality set at the "Cash Disbursement" side is (1, N).

In terms of the cardinalities between events and agents, as mentioned in the revenue cycle, the general case is (1, 1) on the event side and (1, N) on the agent side. In addition, as stated above, we need to illustrate each entity only once in the REA diagram. Figure 1-22 shows the completed REA diagram for Cherokee's expenditure cycle.

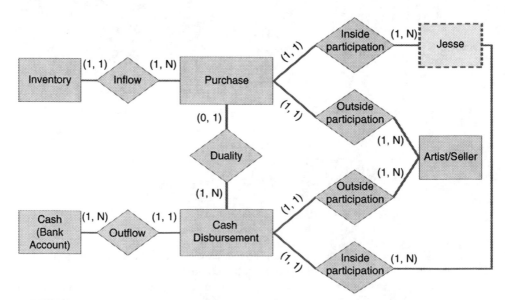

FIGURE 1-22 Complete REA Diagram for Cherokee's Expenditure Cycle

Finally, to make a comprehensive data model for Cherokee, we combine the revenue and expenditure cycle processes as illustrated in the REA diagram in Figure 1-23.

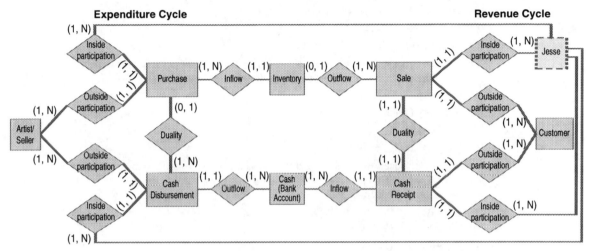

FIGURE 1-23 Comprehensive REA Data Model for Cherokee Art and Antique Store

KEY TERMS

entity	duality	economic resources
relationship	entity-relationship diagram (ERD)	economic events
cardinality	Resource-Event-Agent (REA) data	economic agents
data modeling	model	

QUESTIONS AND PROBLEMS FOR REVIEW

MULTIPLE-CHOICE QUESTIONS

1.1 Which of the following is considered an entity in an REA data model?

(a) Customer

(b) Sale

(c) Finished goods

(d) All of the above are correct.

1.2 A construction company always lets its customers make installment payments. When the company signs a contract with a customer, the customer is required to pay one percent of the total price as down payment. So far, no customer has paid in full at the time of purchase. Which set of cardinalities correctly shows this relationship?

(a) Sales (0, 1) − (1, N) Cash receipts

(b) Sales (1, 1) − (1, N) Cash receipts

(c) Sales (0, N) − (1, 1) Cash receipts

(d) Sales (1, N) − (1, 1) Cash receipts

1.3 A construction company builds custom homes only. So far, none of the customers have ordered two houses at one time. Which set of cardinalities correctly shows the relationship between inventory and sales?

(a) Inventory (0, 1) − (1, 1) Sales

(b) Inventory (1, 1) − (1, 1) Sales

(c) Inventory (1, 1) − (1, N) Sales

(d) Inventory (0, N) − (0, 1) Sales

1.4 A small, local grocery store accepts cash, checks, and credit card payments from customers. The store has no other sources of income. Which set of cardinalities correctly shows the relationship between sales and cash receipts?

(a) Sales (0, 1) − (0, 1) Cash receipts

(b) Sales (1, 1) − (0, 1) Cash receipts

(c) Sales (1, 1) − (1, 1) Cash receipts

(d) Sales (1, N) − (1, 1) Cash receipts

1.5 A large company with several business lines has different types of bank accounts in several banks. Each business line has its own checking account for cash disbursements and cash receipts. Which set of cardinalities correctly shows the relationship between cash (bank accounts) and cash disbursements for the company (not for each business line)?

(a) Cash (0, N) − (0, 1) Cash disbursements

(b) Cash (1, N) − (1, 1) Cash disbursements

(c) Cash (1, 1) − (1, N) Cash disbursements

(d) Cash (1, N) − (1, N) Cash disbursements

1.6 A traditional bookstore just started its e-business using a website to take customer orders, while also maintaining its "brick-and-mortar" store. Which set of cardinalities correctly shows the relationship between sales and salespeople?

(a) Sales (0, 1) − (0, 1) Salespeople

(b) Sales (0, 1) − (1, 1) Salespeople

(c) Sales (0, 1) − (1, N) Salespeople

(d) Sales (1, 1) − (1, N) Salespeople

1.7 A real estate company has many agents buying and selling residential properties and business sites. The company has very high turnover rates for these agents and sometimes agents will leave the company and then return several months later. Which set of cardinalities correctly shows the relationship between sales and agents?

(a) Sales (0, 1) − (0, 1) Agents

(b) Sales (1, 1) − (0, 1) Agents

(c) Sales (1, 1) − (0, N) Agents

(d) Sales (1, 1) − (1, N) Agents

1.8 A retail company would like to store information about current and potential vendors who supply inventories to the company. The company has a choice of vendors from which to purchase any single item of inventory. Which set of cardinalities correctly shows this relationship?

(a) Inventory (1, 1) − (0, N) Vendor

(b) Inventory (1, N) − (1, N) Vendor

(c) Inventory (1, N) − (0, N) Vendor

(d) Inventory (1, N) − (1, 1) Vendor

1.9 Which of the following statements about the REA data model is true?

(a) Each resource is generally linked to at least two agents.

(b) Each event is generally linked to at least three agents.

(c) Each event is generally linked to at least one resource.

(d) Each agent is generally linked to at least two events.

1.10 Which of the following is considered an entity in an REA data model?

(a) Accounts Receivable

(b) Accounts Payable

(c) Fixed Assets

(d) None of the above is correct.

1.11 Which of the following statements is correct?

(a) An ERD always depicts a company's business processes in sequence.

(b) An ERD is conceived to facilitate communication among IT professionals only.

(c) An REA diagram is totally different from an ERD.

(d) The REA model categorizes entities into relationships, events, and agents.

(e) None of the above statements is correct.

1.12 Which of the following would be a common transaction cycle for a pharmaceutical company?

(a) Revenue Cycle

(b) Conversion Cycle

(c) HR Cycle

(d) Financing Cycle

(e) All of the above

PROBLEMS

1.1 Cherokee Art and Antique Store

Develop an REA diagram for Cherokee Art and Antique Store's expenditure cycle to model its purchasing and payment events related to artists/sellers given the following new fact that Jesse likes to collect information on potential artists/sellers for future business. Other situations remain the same.

1.2 Cherokee Art and Antique Store

Develop an REA diagram for Cherokee Art and Antique Store's acquisition activities to model its expenditures related to the purchasing of store furniture, office equipment and other fixed assets only. Assume that Jesse always makes installment payments for asset acquisition. He writes a check for the payment of each asset even if several assets have been purchased from the same vendor, since this way is easier for him to track the unpaid balance of each item. Occasionally, a vendor does **not** require a down payment.

1.3   Cherokee Art and Antique Store

Develop an REA diagram for Cherokee Art and Antique Store's expenditure cycle to model its purchasing and payment events in general (not to include the acquisition event in problem 1.2). That is, other than buying art pieces and paying the artists, Cherokee buys office supplies, orders services for maintenance, pays for other operating expenses such as for water and utility, telephone, and cleaning.

1.4   Carlsbad Surfboards Store

Carlsbad Surfboards Store sells handcrafted surfboards to customers through its network of company salespeople. Each surfboard is given a unique identification number and a suggested selling price when finished.

Upon employment, each salesperson is immediately assigned to service a separate group of customers. When customer data is initially entered into the information system, the customer is immediately assigned to a salesperson. Each sale can include one or more surfboards and can be paid for in any of three ways: (1) immediately in cash (full payments only), (2) on the 15th of the following month (full payments only), or (3) over the course of six months (installments). No more than one salesperson participates in making a particular sale.

Every cash receipt is processed by exactly one of Carlsbad's several cashiers and is deposited into one of Carlsbad's bank accounts. Information about surfboards, employees, and customers often needs to be entered into the database before any transactions involving them have occurred.

Create an REA model for the revenue cycle of Carlsbad Surfboards Store as described.

1.5   Velvet Lounge

Background: Velvet Lounge is a premier upscale nightclub located in the heart of San Francisco. It has two levels which are fully stocked with two bars on each level. Velvet Lounge is richly decorated with velvet furniture, mahogany walls, and giant chandeliers to create a very luxurious lounge.

Velvet Lounge may be entirely rented for hosting an event at a nightclub. Most of the time, the club is rented out for people to host a theme party or an after-party for concerts or other special events. People who tend to rent the entire club are mostly promoters or radio stations. Admission fees are to be determined by the host of the event and all of the admission fees go to the host. This gives the promoters an incentive to bring in a large crowd.

Velvet Lounge has private VIP rooms which may be rented for birthday parties and special occasions on a smaller scale. Depending on the size of the room that is rented, the customer will be given a certain number of VIP guest passes.

Internet Use: Velvet Lounge's official website will enable customers to see upcoming events at the club. The website is used to provide background information about the club to the public. General information such as location and management contact information is posted on the site. Pictures of the club are also posted on the site.

Velvet Lounge's website allows customers to subscribe to its mailing list so they can be notified of special events. This allows Velvet Lounge to keep in touch with its customer base. The mailing list is also used for targeted promotions.

Detailed information about VIP room rentals is available from the website. Customers may submit a request to reserve a VIP room or the entire club through the internet by completing the online form and providing their contact information. Each request will be assigned to a manager who will then check for availability and respond to the customer.

Expenditure Cycle: Velvet Lounge purchases alcohol and other beverages from several vendors. The vendors may provide different products or only one product for the club. Once Velvet Lounge orders from a vendor, the vendor will remain in the database even if the club has not made any recent purchases from the vendor. A purchase can consist of multiple beverage items or it can include only one kind of beverage. All purchase orders must be made by the purchasing manager. Depending on the payment terms with the specific vendors, Velvet's payments may be due in full upon delivery or payments may be due within 30 days of receipt of goods. Either way, only one check is issued per purchase order because payments are always made in full. Only the cashier is authorized to handle cash disbursements and cash receipts. Velvet Lounge uses a single checking account for cash disbursements and cash receipts. All inventories are stored on-site in the stock room of the club.

Revenue Cycle: Velvet Lounge has two sources of income: room rentals and bar service. A customer can rent the entire club or the VIP rooms. Velvet Lounge does not distinguish between the two different customer bases. All rental reservations are initiated by the request of a customer in person or via the telephone, fax, or the internet. Once a reservation request has been received, it will be directed to a manager for approval. The manager assigned to the specific reservation request will check the company database for availability and respond to the customer accordingly. If the room is available, the manager will provide a quote for the customer. When the customer confirms reservation of the room(s), all the necessary contact information of the customer will be entered into the database. Payment in full for the rental is due upon confirmation of the reservation. That is, Velvet Lounge receives one payment for every rental reservation.

Velvet Lounge also serves drinks from its bars. Velvet Lounge has full control of all the bars and retains all of its proceeds. Only staff employees will take drink orders and serve the drinks. Velvet Lounge employees serve at the bar and the VIP rooms. Similarly, all orders must be paid for in full at the time of purchase. However, one customer may "pick up the tab" for other customers (i.e., may pay for several purchases). Again, cashiers are the only employees who handle all the cash receipts from room rentals and drinks purchases.

Required:

1. Construct an REA diagram to depict Velvet Lounge's revenue cycle.

2. Construct an REA diagram to depict Velvet Lounge's expenditure cycle.

1.6 Worifree Properties, Inc.

Background: Worifree Properties is a small start-up company that came into existence in the spring of 2005 with a total of six employees. Headquartered in San Jose, California, the company has experienced moderate growth despite uncertain economic times. Its core business focuses on property management. Worifree performs all property management-related tasks to satisfy the needs of its clients. Its clients are real estate investors/owners who are interested in renting out their property without incurring the work and worry associated with its management. Worifree attempts to reduce owner involvement in the management process as much as possible while providing them with accurate and reliable services and accounting.

Worifree's clients own one or more properties in the Bay area. Although a property may have more than one owner, most multiple owners are married couples. In those cases, Worifree keeps track of only one of the owners. Worifree performs rent collection, maintenance, and advertising, and prepares contracts on behalf of the real estate owners for leasing transactions. Maintenance and advertising services are all outsourced to contractors, while lease handling and other services are managed by internal employees. All cash inflows and outflows are controlled through one bank account, although Worifree has a couple of accounts with Bank United. In addition, because the company has so few employees, many transactions are handled online via electronic funds transfers. For example, Worifree agrees to electronically forward the rental income to corresponding owners immediately upon receiving them from the tenant(s). All tenants are required to make rental payments to Worifree using electronic funds transfers.

Revenue Cycle: Worifree's revenue is from one source only–real estate owners. A revenue transaction is recorded strictly for services performed by Worifree's employees or its contractors on one property. Contractor services include those for maintenance and advertising on clients' properties. The contractor's invoice Worifree for services performed on a particular occasion may include one or more services. Once the contractors are paid, Worifree, in turn, invoices the property owners with a service invoice for the expenditures. Worifree invoices its clients for the same amount as the contractors invoice Worifree.

Included in Worifree's service invoice is a monthly property management fee and charges for other services performed by its employees, such as new rental lease arrangements and maintenance expenditures. An invoice involves only one employee, but an employee may be involved in more than one invoice. Service invoices are prepared for each client every month and the client is required to pay in full for each bill. On rare occasions, some clients may not pay on time and Worifree accepts late payments with finance charges. Worifree maintains only current clients' information in its database. The cash collections are done through electronic funds transfer; thus, no employee is involved in the cash collection process.

Expenditure Cycle: The expenditure cycle of Worifree is not complex. There are two kinds of expenditures: (1) services provided by contractors and (2) supplies/fixed assets purchased from vendors. Maintenance and advertising services are provided by a specified set of vendors for quality and cost control. Since Worifree always gets services from contractors with whom they have had transactions before, there could be a delay to get the desired service when certain contractors are busy. Some contractors provide more than one kind of service for Worifree. When each service is completed and Worifree is billed, Worifree always pays the contractor electronically in full.

When making purchases, Worifree refers to the list of qualified vendors. Some vendors in the vendor list are alternate vendors. Worifree orders from the alternate vendors only if the regular vendor does not have a specific item in stock. All purchases are made by purchasing agents. Each purchase involves only one purchasing agent and one vendor. Vendors may provide Worifree one or more than one type of product on more than one occasion. Payments for most purchases are made in full. Some vendors bill Worifree monthly, particularly for office supplies. However, when purchasing expensive office equipment or large furniture, Worifree makes installment payments. Since Worifree has an excellent credit history, some vendors do not require a down payment for installment purchases.

Required:

1. Construct an REA diagram to depict Worifree's revenue cycle.
2. Construct an REA diagram to depict Worifree's expenditure cycle.

CHAPTER 2

DATA MODELS AND RELATIONAL DATABASES

INTRODUCTION

The database development process begins with **enterprise modeling** to set the range and general contents of organizational databases as presented in Chapter 1. The example of an enterprise model is reproduced in Figure 2-1 for a review.

Then, in the stage of **conceptual data modeling**, the requirements of the overall entities are identified and analyzed based on transaction cycles. For example, Figure 2-2 is a conceptual data model for Cherokee's revenue and expenditure cycles as discussed in Chapter 1.

This chapter is concerning **logical database design**. Logical database design is the process of transforming the conceptual data model into a logical data model. The logical data models used in this chapter are relational databases. Most information systems today are based on relational databases, the most popular type of databases used for transaction processing.

The purpose of this chapter is to expand on our discussion in Chapter 1 using the business-process-based data models to design a relational database. This chapter presents important concepts and definitions of relational databases. In addition, the database normalization processes are explained. Through these processes, we can determine whether a database table is properly designed and how to minimize data redundancy and possible anomalies in a database table. Upon completion of this chapter, you should be able, based on a data model, to accomplish the following:

- Identify primary and foreign keys for each entity and relationship in the data model,
- Create tables that are linked properly with foreign keys or through relationship table(s),
- Examine whether a database table design has anomalies, and
- Normalize a table to the third normal form.

RELATIONAL DATABASES

Basic Concepts and Definitions

A database is an organized collection of logically related data that[1] are stored in tables (or files). There are three main constructs of the structure of a relational database. The primary construct is called a **relation** or a **table** that is a storage structure with rows and columns

---

[1]Data are facts, text, graphics, and images that can be recorded and stored on computer media, such as customer names, logos, and addresses. Information is data that has been processed and organized in such a way that it can increase the knowledge of decision makers, such as a report with the due date and accounts receivable balance of each customer.

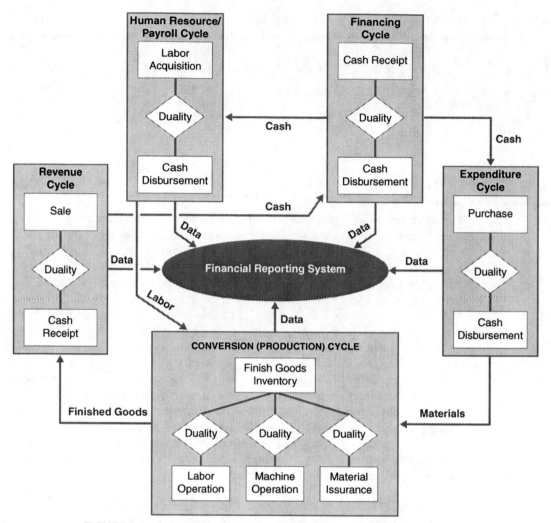

FIGURE 2-1 Overall REA Model for an Accounting Information System

much like a spreadsheet. Each table in a database represents either an entity, or a relationship between entities (i.e., a relationship table). Tables need to be properly linked to make a relational database. The **columns** in a table are called **fields** that represent the **attributes** or characteristics of the entity or relationship. The **rows** in a table are called **records** or **tuples** that represent all the specific data values associated with one instance.

In Chapter 1, using an REA diagram, we created the data model for Cherokee's revenue cycle. This data model is repeated in Figure 2-3.

When we convert an REA diagram to a database, each entity becomes a table. Therefore, according to Figure 2-3, Cherokee's revenue cycle database consists of the following five tables: Inventory Table, Cash Table, Sale Table, Cash Receipt Table and Customer Table. Recall from Chapter 1 that we do not need to track information about

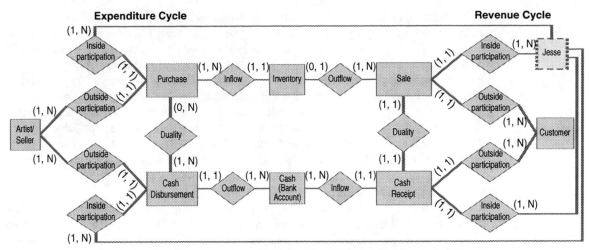

FIGURE 2-2 Comprehensive REA Data Model for Cherokee Art and Antique Store

Jesse since he is the only person conducting sales. Therefore, it is not necessary to have a table to store data about Jesse. If there were more than one salesperson, it would be necessary to create a Salesperson Table in the model. In general, we need to create a table for each entity in the REA diagram to store data important to the company.

Each column of a table represents an attribute (or characteristic) of its entity. For example, the attributes for the Customer Table may include Customer ID, Customer Name, Customer Address, Customer City, Customer State, Customer ZIP Code, Customer Phone Number and Customer Email. Each row of a table represents an instance (or a record) of the entity. That is, one specific row in the Customer Table provides all the data values for one specific customer.

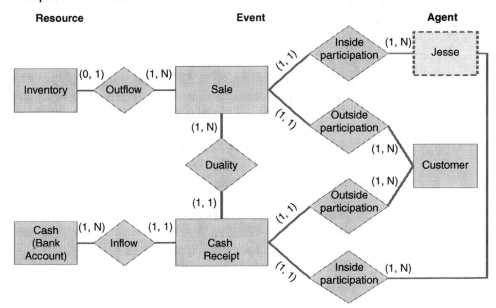

FIGURE 2-3 Complete REA Diagram for Cherokee's Revenue Cycle

A **primary key** attribute is a **unique** identifier of each instance of an entity. For example, the primary key of the Customer Table is Customer ID. Customer Name would not be an appropriate primary key unless Jesse is *absolutely* sure that he does not and will not ever have customers with the same name, which is a practical impossibility.

A **foreign key** is an attribute included in one table that is the primary key in another table. We use foreign keys to link tables. For example, the Cash Receipt Table may include attributes such as Cash Receipt #, Date, Amount, and Customer ID. By including the Customer ID (the primary key of the Customer Table) in the Cash Receipt Table, we can link the Cash Receipt Table and the Customer Table to obtain data for decision making purposes. For example, we can easily link a cash receipt record to its associated customer and extract information about the specific customer on that record. The Customer ID in the Cash Receipt Table in this example is called a foreign key.

Another example of using a foreign key would be including the primary key of the Inventory Table, "Item #," as an attribute in the Sale Table. "Item #" in the Sale Table then would be a foreign key, providing a link between the Inventory Table and the Sale Table.

We can use cardinalities in the REA diagram discussed in Chapter 1 to determine the relationships between the entities in terms of a relational database. We do this by referring to the maximum cardinality on each side of the relation in the REA diagram. Since we know that a maximum cardinality can be a 1 or an N, we have three possible relationships. A one-to-one (1:1) relationship occurs when a record (row) in a table relates to a record in another table once and only once. A one-to-many (1:N) relationship occurs when a record in a table can relate to several records in another table. A many-to-many (N:N) relationship occurs when several records in a table relate to several records in another table.

Basic Requirements of Tables

The relational database approach imposes some requirements on the structure of tables. If these basic requirements are not fulfilled or if data redundancy exists in a database, problems (called anomalies) may occur. The requirements include the following:

- **The Entity Integrity Rule:** Each table in a relational database must have a primary key attribute, and it must have a value for each record (i.e., it cannot be null).
- **The Referential Integrity Rule:** We use foreign keys to link tables so the corresponding values must match each other. To properly link the data in related tables, a value for a foreign key attribute must either be null or match one of the data values that corresponds to the value of a primary key attribute in another table.
- **Each attribute must be uniquely named**.
- **Values of a specific attribute must be of the same type.** In other words, if a column (attribute) is designated as text, numeric, or currency, all the data contained in that specific column must follow the designated data type. For example, data in a column designated as currency must all be in dollars and cents format. Therefore, the column could not contain numeric data representing percentages nor could there be text data.
- **Each attribute (column) of a record (row or tuple) must be single-data-valued.** This requirement forces us to create a relationship table for each many-to-many relationship.

For example, for a grocery store, the relationship between the entities of "inventory" and "sale" is often a many-to-many relationship, as indicated in Figure 2-4. That is, each kind

FIGURE 2-4 Inventory-Sales Relationship

of inventory could be sold many times, and the store may sell different kinds of inventory in one transaction. If we include the attribute of "Item #" in the Sale Table as a foreign key so that we know which items are sold, each sale record may have **several** values for the attribute of "Item #," which violates the requirement that each attribute of a record must be single-data-valued. A similar problem occurs when we try to use "Sale #" as a foreign key in the Inventory Table. Therefore, we must create an additional table, a **relationship table**, to link two tables with a many-to-many relationship.

In Figure 2-4, the relationship table is called the Line Item Table (in the diamond-shaped relationship symbol). This Line Item Table is used to link the Inventory Table and the Sales Table. Recall that each sale may include many kinds of inventory items. To uniquely identify each record of the Line Item Table, the primary key of this Line Item Table must be a two-column attribute that includes both Sale # and Item # to link the Inventory Table and the Sales Table without having multiple data values in each cell. The primary key in a relationship table is always a combined key, composed of the primary keys from tables in the relationship. This is called a concatenated primary key (also called a composite key).

An example in Microsoft Access is shown in Figure 2-5. The symbol of "∞" in Access means many.

- All other attributes (columns) in a table must describe a characteristic of the entity identified by the primary key. For example, including customer address or phone number as an attribute in the Cash Receipt Table would be incorrect. To link to this

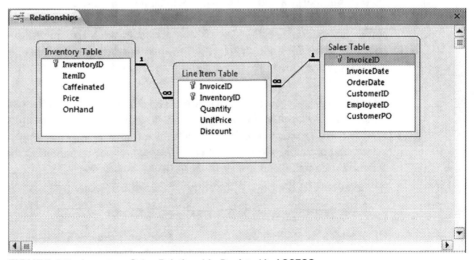

FIGURE 2-5 Inventory-Sales Relationship Depicted in ACCESS

information, you would include Customer ID in the table as a foreign key but since neither customer address nor phone number is a characteristic of the cash receipt event, they must not be included in the Cash Receipt Table.

The sequence of attributes or records in a table is of no importance.

Steps of Implementing an REA Diagram in a Relational Database

We will use the same example in Chapter 1, Cherokee Art and Antique Store, to illustrate how to implement an REA diagram in a relational database.

Step 1:   Create a table for each entity.

According to Cherokee's REA data model in Figure 2-2, we need to create following eight tables for the entities: Inventory Table, Cash Table, Sale Table, Cash Receipt Table, Purchase Table, Cash Disbursement Table, Artist/Seller Table (which we will refer to as Artist Table from now on), and Customer Table. Notice that the title of each table should be the same as the name of the entity it represents to make it easier to refer back to the original data model design as appeared in the REA diagram.

Step 2:   Create a table for each many-to-many relationship.

One relationship table is needed for the many-to-many (N:N) relationship between the events of "Purchase" and "Cash Disbursement" (i.e., Duality 1). To make it easy to understand, we name this relationship table Purchase-Cash Disbursement. In addition, the name of the relationship on the REA diagram should also be renamed as Purchase-Cash Disbursement.

Step 3:   Examine tables with a one-to-one relationship.

We need to examine the entities with a one-to-one relationship carefully because they often should be collapsed into one entity. Since all sales are paid for immediately in cash, Cherokee has a one-to-one (1:1) relationship between the events "Sales" and "Cash Receipt." The sales data Cherokee might need would include a primary key (e.g., sales invoice number), sales date (which would be the same as cash receipt date), dollar amount, and type of payment such as cash, check or debit card. Therefore, we can collapse the two tables into one table called Sales Table. However, such a relationship would also suggest that Cherokee does not obtain cash receipts from any source other than its sales so this decision would need to be thought over carefully. When such a decision is made, Cherokee's REA model should also be modified accordingly.

Step 4:   Identify the attributes and assign the primary key for each table.

There are several ways to present a table structure. The table structure adopted here is a simple form in which a table's attributes are enclosed in parentheses following the table name, and a double underline indicates the primary key column(s).[2] Based on Cherokee's REA data model, its table structures are listed as follows:

Inventory Table (<u>Item #</u>, Inventory Description, Inventory Cost)

Cash Table (<u>Account #</u>, Account Type, Balance)

Sales Table (<u>Sale #</u>, Sale Date, Sale Amount, Payment Type)

---

[2]There are other conventions for indicating keys. For example, a primary key and a foreign key could be identified using a single underline and an asterisk, respectively. Alternatively, the primary key can be identified as (PK) and each foreign key can be identified as (FK).

Purchase Table (<u>Purchase #</u>, Purchase Date, Purchase Amount)

Cash Disbursement Table (<u>Check #</u>, Check Date, Payment Amount)

Artist Table (<u>Artist ID</u>, Artist Name, Artist Address, Artist Phone #, Artist Email)

Customer Table (<u>Customer ID</u>, Customer Name, Customer Address, Customer
City, Customer State, Customer ZIP Code, Customer Phone #,
Customer Email)

Purchase-Cash Disbursement Table (<u>Purchase #</u>, <u>Check #</u>)

Step 5: Implement relationships using foreign keys.

The last step is to link tables using foreign keys. In our table structure, we use a single underline to indicate a foreign key. If there are necessary tables with a one-to-one relationship (those that should not be collapsed into one table), it does not matter which table's primary key becomes the foreign key in the other table, but do not post both primary keys as foreign keys (i.e., one in each table).

However, the primary key of the table with a one-to-many (1:N) relationship always becomes the foreign key in the one-to-one (1,1) entity's table. That way, we can make sure that each attribute of a record is single-valued for both tables. For example, to link the **Artist Table** with the **Purchase Table**, we add **Artist ID** to the **Purchase Table** as a foreign key, since each purchase transaction involves only one artist. The revised table structure of the **Purchase Table** is as follows:

Purchase Table (<u>Purchase #</u>, Purchase Date, Purchase Amount, <u>Artist ID</u>).
After determining the proper foreign keys, other revised table structures are listed as follow:

Inventory Table (<u>Item #</u>, Inventory Description, Inventory Cost, Purchase #, Sale #)

Sale Table (<u>Sale #</u>, Sale Date, Sale Amount, Payment Type, Customer ID, Account #)

Cash Disbursement Table (<u>Check #</u>, Disbursement Date, Payment Amount,
Artist ID, Account #)

The revised REA diagram, with table structures, is presented in Figure 2-6.

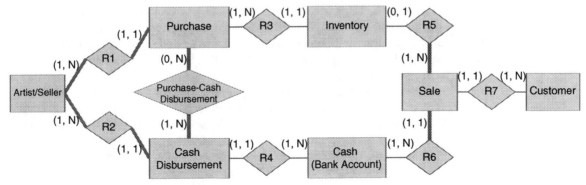

FIGURE 2-6 Cherokee's Revised REA Data Model

Inventory Table (<u>Item #</u>, Inventory Description, Inventory Cost, Purchase #, Sale #)

Cash Table (<u>Account #</u>, Account Type, Balance)

Sale Table (<u>Sale #</u>, Sale Date, Sale Amount, Payment Type, Customer ID, Account #)

Purchase Table (<u>Purchase #</u>, Purchase Date, Purchase Amount, Artist ID)

Cash Disbursement Table (<u>Check #</u>, Disbursement Date, Payment Amount, Artist ID, Account #)

Artist Table (<u>Artist ID</u>, Artist Name, Artist Address, Artist City, Artist State, Artist ZIP Code, Artist Phone #, Artist Email)

Customer Table (<u>Customer ID</u>, Customer Name, Customer Address, Customer City, Customer State, Customer ZIP Code, Customer Phone #, Customer Email)

Purchase-Cash Disbursement Table (<u>Purchase #</u>, <u>Check #</u>)

DATABASE ANOMALIES AND NORMALIZATION

Basic Concepts and Definitions

During logical data modeling, we often use general business knowledge and the understanding of the specific company to determine which attributes should be included in different tables. In general, after using the proper steps to create an REA data model (the logical design), the design of a database should not contain any serious flaws. However, before proceeding with physical design, we may want to validate the logical design. Normalization is a tool to validate and improve a logic design to satisfy database requirements and to avoid unnecessary duplication of data. It is the process of decomposing tables with anomalies to produce well-structured (often smaller) tables. Note that, however, normalization may result in slower processes in some cases. For example, if one table is normalized into three different tables, an application program that needs to extract data from the original table would need to access three tables for when queries are made. Hence, the application program could be slower than before.

Three anomalies may occur when a table is not well designed. The **update anomaly** causes problems in updating a record. That is, updating a data value of one record will have to take place in multiple rows. Data inconsistency may occur due to this anomaly as the update must be done many times and a record may be missed. The **insert anomaly** causes difficulty, often impossibility, to insert new data into a table. The **delete anomaly** involves unintended loss of data that arises when deleting a row in a table. The following vendor table showing data from part of its entire table is used to explain these anomalies. The logical design of this original table presented in Figure 2-7 is: **Vendor Table 1** (<u>Vendor#</u>, Vendor Name, Vendor Address, Contact Name, Phone#, <u>Item#</u>, Description, Unit Price).

Since Vendor# is the primary key of this table, adding and deleting records should be based on Vendor#. This vendor table has update anomalies. For example, if we want to update the description of item K-8 from DVD player to Sony DVD, we have to search the

Vendor#	Vendor Name	Vendor Address	Contact Name	Phone#	Item#	Description	Unit Price
2010	AXA, Inc.	22 Heaven Wood Drive	Annie White	234-3435	M-45	Blender	$15.99
					K-4	iPod	$65.00
2011	Sys Co.	2273 Morgan Street	John Doe	655-7512	D-12	LCD projector	$560.00
2012	MFS	46 Kings Square, #5	Rachelle Brown	234-7799	M-45	Blender	$18.00
					K-4	iPod	$63.80
2013	Lazard	8 Santa Ana	Ed King	734-0109	K-8	DVD player	$134.00
2014	XYZ Co.	19 Columbus	Lan Lee	878-1888	K-8	DVD player	$129.99

FIGURE 2-7 Partial Data in a Vendor Table

entire table to find and change every occurrence of that description from DVD player to Sony DVD. Overlooking one row would create inconsistency in the database. This table also has insert anomalies. For example, if the company explored a few new models of iPods and would like to enter the information into the database, it is not possible until the company finds a vendor carrying the new models and inserts that vendor into the database. This is because the primary key of the table is Vendor#. According to the entity integrity rule, the primary key cannot be null. That is, without specific information of a vendor, we cannot insert any inventory data. The worst anomaly is the delete anomaly. Assume that Sys Co., one of the company's vendors listed above, went out of business. If we delete its records (Vendor#: 2011 and Vendor Name: Sys Co.) from the database, we would accidentally delete the inventory information for the LCD projectors if Sys Co. is the only one selling LCD projectors to the company.

Steps in Normalization

Normalization can be understood and accomplished in stages. Each stage corresponds to a normal form. In this book, we describe and illustrate the steps to reach first, second, and third normal forms. Although not discussed in this book, the fifth normal form is often deemed to be the highest level of normalization in which any remaining anomalies are removed.

Step 1: Remove any repeating groups (First Normal Form).
Any repeating groups must be separated into a different table to reach the first normal form. Repeating groups are those related attributes with multi-valued data. In the above-mentioned vendor table, inventory information of item#, description, and unit price is a repeating group as these columns have multi-valued data. That is, multiple data values are associated with the same primary key (e.g., two items associated with vendor# 2010 and 2021). Hence, to normalize the vendor table to first normal form, we need to decompose **Vendor Table 1** into two tables: **Vendor Table 2** and **Inventory Table**.

According to Figure 2-7, the attribute of Unit Price is both vendor and item specific. Hence, we need to tentatively exclude this attribute from both tables so that they can reach the first normal form without repeating groups. After Step 1, the logical designs of the two tables are: **Vendor Table 2** (Vendor#, Vendor Name, Vendor Address, Contact Name, Phone#), and **Inventory Table** (Item#, Description).

Step 2:   Remove any partial dependencies (Second Normal Form).

When we normalize a table, we need to make sure that the decomposed tables are linked properly so data can be retrieved from them. Tentatively, let's use Item# with Vendor# in the vendor table as a concatenated key so we can add back the attribute of Unit Price to the new vendor table. This proposed table has a logical design as follows: **Vendor Table 3** (<u>Vendor#</u>, <u>Item#</u>, Vendor Name, Vendor Address, Contact Name, Phone#, Unit Price).

This proposed table has the problem of partial dependency. **Partial dependency** exists if any non-key attribute[3] is dependent on part, not all, of the primary key. That is, Vendor Name, Vendor Address, Contact Name, Phone# are functionally dependent on Vendor# only, which is only part of the concatenated primary key, not both Vendor# and Item#. Only Unit Price is dependent on the whole primary key: Vendor# and Item#. Hence, we need to decompose **Vendor Table 3** into two tables: **Vendor Table 4** (<u>Vendor#</u>, Vendor Name, Vendor Address, Contact Name, Phone#), and **Vendor-Inventory Table** (<u>Vendor#</u>, <u>Item#</u>, Unit Price). The **Vendor-Inventory Table** is a relationship table to link the **Inventory Table** and **Vendor Table 4**. Examining Figure 2-7 again, we know that the relationship between the entities (i.e., vendor and inventory) is many-to-many. As we mentioned earlier, whenever there is a many-to-many relationship, we must use a relationship table to link the two entities; otherwise, the tables cannot be normalized.

Step 3:   Remove any transitive dependencies (Third Normal Form).

A **transitive dependency** refers to a functional dependency between two or more non-key attributes in the same table. Referring to Figure 2-7, the attribute Description is dependent on a non-key attribute (Item#), not the primary key (Vendor#), although Item# is dependent upon Vendor#. This is a case of transitive dependency. After our first two steps of normalization, we have already removed transitive dependency from the original table design. Our final results of normalization are three tables:

> **Inventory Table** (<u>Item#</u>, Description)
>
> **Vendor Table 4** (<u>Vendor#</u>, Vendor Name, Vendor Address, Contact Name, Phone#)
>
> **Vendor-Inventory Table** (<u>Vendor#</u>, <u>Item#</u>, Unit Price)

Summary of Normalization

Normalization is a formal process to determine which attributes should be grouped together in a table. It validates the logical design to avoid any violation of database requirements that cause data redundancy and database anomalies. Normalization is done by decomposing a table with anomalies into smaller, well-structured tables. A table is in first normal form (1NF) if it contains no repeating groups (multi-valued attributes). A table is in second normal form (2NF) if it satisfies the requirement of first normal form and if every non-key attribute is fully dependent on the primary key. Finally, a table is in third normal form (3NF) if it satisfies the requirement of second normal form and if all the non-key attributes are independent from each other (i.e., no transitive dependency). Any table that satisfies the third normal form will not have any update anomalies, insert anomalies, or delete anomalies.

---

[3]Non-key attributes are those attributes that are not the primary key.

KEY TERMS

primary key	concatenated/composite key	insertion anomaly
foreign key	relationship table	deletion anomaly
entity integrity rule	normalization	third normal form
referential integrity rule	update anomaly	

QUESTIONS AND PROBLEMS FOR REVIEW

MULTIPLE-CHOICE QUESTIONS

2.1 In designing a database, what is the referential integrity rule?

(a) The primary key in a table should not be null.

(b) The foreign key in a table should not be null.

(c) Each table must have a primary key and a foreign key.

(d) Two of the above are correct.

(e) None of the above is correct.

2.2 In designing a database, what is the entity integrity rule?

(a) The primary key in a table should not be null.

(b) The foreign key in a table should not be null.

(c) Each table must have a primary key and a foreign key.

(d) Two of the above are correct.

(e) None of the above is correct.

2.3 Which table would logically have repeating groups?

(a) **Student Table** (Student ID, Student Name, Major, GPA)

(b) **Student Table** (Student ID, Student Name, Major, Courses Taken)

(c) **Student Table** (Student ID, Student Name, Major, Faculty Advisor)

(d) Two of the above are correct.

(e) None of the above is correct.

2.4 Which table has transitive dependency?

(a) **Student Table** (Student ID, Student Name, Major, Courses Taken, Grade)

(b) **Student Table** (Student ID, Student Name, Major, Course#, Course Title, Grade)

(c) **Student Table** (Student ID, Student Name, Major, Faculty Advisor, Faculty Office#)

(d) Two of the above are correct.

(e) None of the above is correct.

2.5 How many tables are necessary to build a database according to the following data model?

(a) 6

(b) 7

(c) 8

(d) 9

(e) 10

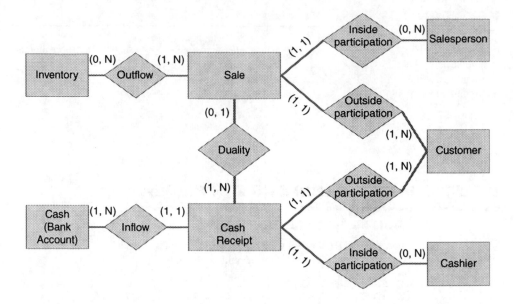

2.6   Which of the following describes the right order of implementing an REA diagram in a relational database?

I.   Create a table for each entity

II. Link tables using foreign keys

III. Identify attributes and assign the primary key for each table

(a) I – II – III

(b) I – III – II

(c) III – II – I

(d) II – I – III

2.7   Which of the following table designs would most likely cause the **update anomaly**?

(a) Artist (<u>Artist ID</u>, Name, Email, Date of Birth, Awards received)

(b) Inventory-Warehouse (<u>Item #</u>, <u>Warehouse name</u>, Warehouse Manager Name, Number of Items)

(c) Vendor-Inventory (<u>Vendor ID</u>, <u>Item #</u>, Unit Price, Item Description)

(d) Two of the above will cause the update anomaly.

Below is a sample relational database table for a bookstore. The ISBN# is the primary key of the table. Answer questions 2.8 and 2.9 based on the information provided in the table.

ISBN #	Book Title	Year	Publishing Company	Publisher Contact
8175257660	20th Anniversary	2012	ABC Publishing	Adam Hefner
8175268101	If I Ask You	2009	XYZ Publishing	John Lee
8175266050	Gold Mine	2011	XYZ Publishing	John Lee

2.8 Which anomaly(ies) may be caused by the table design?

(a) Update anomaly only

(b) Update and delete anomalies

(c) Insert and delete anomalies

(d) Update, insert, and delete anomalies

(e) None of the above is correct

2.9 Assume that ISBN# is assigned to each edition of a book. Upon completion of required normalization steps, how many well-designed tables will exist?

(a) 4

(b) 3

(c) 2

(d) 1

Below is a partial relational database table for a movie producer. Answer questions 2.10 and 2.11 based on the information provided in the table.

Movie Title	Theater Name	Number of Plays	Movie Director
<u>Inside Man</u>	<u>AMC Tyler Galleria</u>	825	Spike Lee
<u>Pirates of the Caribbean</u>	<u>UltraStar Chula Vista</u>	32	Rob Marshall
<u>Shark</u>	<u>Edwards Mira Mesa Stadium 18</u>	1048	Spike Lee
<u>Lucky Number Slevin</u>	<u>AMC Mission Valley 18</u>	671	Paul McGuigan

Note:* Primary key is indicated as double-underlined.

2.10 Which issue exists about the table design?

(a) Partial dependency

(b) Transitive dependency

(c) Partial dependency and transitive dependency

(d) No problem with the table design

2.11 Assume that the movie producer would like to add the location of each theater into the database. Upon completion of required normalization steps, how many well-designed tables will exist?

(a) 1

(b) 2

(c) 3

(d) 4

2.12 Which of the following table designs would least likely violate the first normal form?

(a) Professor (<u>Professor ID</u>, Name, Phone Number, <u>Course Title</u>, Age)

(b) Student (<u>Student ID</u>, Name, Address, Degree Earned, Admission Year)

(c) Inventory (<u>Item#</u>, Description, Unit Cost, <u>Purchasing Agent ID</u>, <u>Warehouse Name</u>)

(d) Sale (<u>Sale#</u>, Date, Sale Amount, <u>Item#</u>, Description)

2.13 Normalization is performed in order to:

(a) minimize data redundancy in a database table.

(b) improve efficiency of a database and its associated applications' operations.

(c) minimize data anomalies in a database table.

(d) a and c

(e) a, b, and c

2.14 Which of the following describes the right order for the database development process?

I. Identify and analyze the general structure of the organizational databases based on a group of associated transactions.

II. Consider the requirements between related entities and determine the cardinalities.

III. Transform the REA diagram into database tables.

IV. Identify the overall entities in each transaction cycle.

(a) I – II – III – IV

(b) I – III – II – IV

(c) I – IV – II – III

(d) II – I – III – IV

(e) II – III – I – IV

PROBLEMS

2.1 Creating an REA Diagram based on given tables

Examine the following tables and indicate the primary key (using PK) and the foreign key(s) (using FK) for each table. Based on the given tables, draw a **complete** REA diagram for the database.

Inventory				
Item_No	Description	Unit Cost	Unit Price	QOH
2010	Blender	14.00	29.95	100
2015	Toaster	12.00	19.95	200
2020	Mixer	23.00	33.95	150
2025	Television	499.00	699.95	95
2030	Freezer	799.00	999.95	52
2035	Refrigerator	699.00	849.95	75
2040	Radio	45.00	79.95	200
2045	Clock	79.00	99.95	150

Salesperson	
Salesperson_No	Salesperson_Name
101	John Smith
102	Brenda Kim
103	Julia Berens
104	Joe McGuire

Cashier	
Cashier_No	Name
201	Scott Brown
202	Stony Lee
203	Jim White
204	Pat Thomas

Customer

Customer_No	Name	City	State	Credit_Limit
1000	Smith	Phoenix	AZ	2500
1001	Jones	St. Louis	MO	1500
1002	Jeffries	Atlanta	GA	4000
1003	Gilkey	Phoenix	AZ	5000
1004	Lankford	Phoenix	AZ	2000
1005	Zeile	Chicago	IL	2000
1006	Pagnozzi	Salt Lake	UT	3000
1007	Arocha	Chicago	IL	1000

Sales

Invoice_No	Date	Salesperson_No	Customer_No	Amount
101	4/03/2006	101	1000	1549.90
102	4/05/2006	103	1003	299.85
103	4/05/2006	103	1002	1449.80
104	4/15/2006	104	1000	799.90
105	4/15/2006	102	1005	849.95
106	4/16/2006	102	1007	99.95
107	5/02/2006	101	1002	2209.70
108	5/03/2006	103	1000	799.90

Sales-Inventory

Invoice_No	Item_No	Quantity	Extension
101	1025	1	699.95
101	1035	1	849.95
102	1045	3	299.85
103	1010	1	29.95
103	1015	1	19.95
103	1025	2	1399.95
104	1025	1	699.95
104	1045	1	99.95
105	1035	1	849.95
106	1045	1	99.95
107	1030	1	999.95
107	1035	1	849.95
107	1040	2	159.90
107	1045	2	199.90
108	1025	1	699.95
108	1045	1	99.95

Cash Collections					
Remittance_No	Date	Amount	Invoice_No	Cashier_No	Customer_No
220	5/02/2006	1549.90	101	203	1000
278	5/10/2006	799.90	108	202	1000
276	5/30/2006	2209.70	107	202	1002
289	5/30/2006	849.95	105	204	1005

2.2 Cardinalities

Considering each business situation, indicate the maximum and minimum cardinalities for the following events. The first one is done for you.

Business situations	Cardinalities	
	Sales	Cash collections
1. Cash sales	(1, 1)	(1, 1)
2. Installment sales for firms like car dealers; down payment is required.		
3. The company often has credit sales. Customers must pay the full amount for each transaction.		
	Sales	Inventory
4. A regular retail store that sells low-cost, mass-produced items and often carries new items.		
5. A construction company that builds custom homes only.		

2.3 ABC Company—Identify Entities and the Primary/Foreign keys

Examine the following database. In the Entity column, indicate whether the Table name represents a Resource, Event, Agent or Relationship by using the following notations: "R" for Resource, "E" for Event, "A" for Agent, and "Relationship" for Relationship (i.e., if the table is used to link two tables having a many-to-many relationship). Double underline the primary key and underline the foreign key(s) in the attributes column for each table. Not all tables have foreign key(s).

Entity	Table Name	Attributes
	Receive goods	InvReceipt#, date, condition of goods, SSN# (for receiving clerk), carrier
	Order goods	PO#, date, expected receiving date, total amount, vendor#, SSN# (for purchasing clerk)
	Receive – Inventory	InvReceipt#, item#, quantity
	Inventory	Item#, description, standard unit cost, list price
	Cash	account#, bank ID, bank address, balance
	Request goods	Requisition#, date, date needed, vendor#, PO#, requesting supervisor, SSN# (for purchasing clerk#)
	Pay for goods	check#, date, amount, vendor#, account#, InvReceipt#, SSN# (for cashier)
	Request – Inventory	Requisition#, item#, quantity
	Order – Inventory	PO#, item#, actual unit cost, quantity
	Employee	SSN#, name, address, phone, etc.
	Order – Receive	PO#, InvReceipt#
	Vendor	vendor#, name, address, contact person, phone, fax, email

2.4 Carlsbad Surfboards Store

Carlsbad Surfboards Store sells handcrafted surfboards to customers through its network of company salespeople. Each surfboard is given a unique identification number and a suggested selling price when finished.

Upon employment, each salesperson is immediately assigned to service a separate group of customers. When customer data is initially entered into the information system, the customer is immediately assigned to a salesperson. Each sale can include one or more surfboards and can be paid for in any of three ways: (1) immediately in cash (full payments only), (2) on the 15th of the following month (full payments only), or (3) over the course of six months as installments. No more than one salesperson participates in making a particular sale.

Every cash receipt is processed by exactly one of Carlsbad's several cashiers and is deposited into one of Carlsbad's bank accounts. Information about surfboards, employees, and customers often needs to be entered into the database before any transactions involving them have occurred.

The following data items (attributes) are of interest to potential users of this model:

Surfboard-id#	Cash-account-balance
Customer-name	Cash-receipt#
Salesperson-name	Cashier-name
Cash-receipt-total-amount	Description-of-surfboard
Sale-total-amount	List-price-for-a-surfboard
Sale#	Salesperson#
Cash-account#	Cash-account-type
Customer#	Cashier#
Cash-receipt-amount-applied-to-a-sale	

Based on the REA model you created in Problem 1.4 and the attributes provided above, create a paper database for Carlsbad Surfboards Store.

2.5 Normalize a wholesale company's database

Given below is the design of a Sales table for a wholesale company. Please indicate the primary key and possible foreign keys for the table. Given the current design of this table, list two violations of the basic requirements of a relational data model. Indicate possible anomalies in the table and then normalize the table to third normal form.

SO#	Invoice Date	Item #	Description	Quantity Ordered	Unit Price	Customer#	Customer Name
101	7/5/2006	2033	Washer	5	$359.99	22	Brown Co.
		2051	Drier	8	$372.00		
102	7/5/2006	1099	TV	4	$258.00	26	Homebase
103	7/6/2006	2028	VCR	10	$179.99	24	Easy Shop
		2034	CD player	10	$185.00		
		2045	DVD player	5	$200.00		
104	7/8/2000	1099	TV	15	$258.00	22	Brown Co.

2.6 Normalize a library's database

Given below is the table of data for a library. First, determine which attribute is the best primary key. Second, examine the table and indicate the anomalies that may occur with the original design of this database? Why? Third, normalize the table into the third normal form to prepare it for use in a relational database environment.

Call#	Title	Borrower ID#	First Name	Last Name	Date Out	Date Due
K561.02	Soccer	S551442	John	Austin	12-03-12	01-03-13
D221.67	US Presidents	S702361	James	Wilson	12-20-12	01-20-13
I264.89	HR Laws & Regulations	F012618	Mark	Ding	12-20-12	03-20-13
H122.34	Volcanoes	S702361	James	Wilson	12-20-12	01-20-13
K249.02	Swimming	S002579	Freddie	Sunder	01-03-13	02-03-13
M426.52	Egypt	S002579	Freddie	Sunder	01-03-13	02-03-13
K922.4	Badminton	F012618	Mark	Ding	01-05-13	04-05-13

2.7 Quest, Inc.

The following tables and attributes exist in a relational database of Quest, Inc. (1) Draw a complete REA diagram for this database. **You must include cardinalities.** Determine the proper cardinalities based on the given design of each table and the additional information. (2) Indicate any errors that exist in the given database design by providing a proper table structure.

Table	Attributes
Vendor	Vendor#, Name, Address, City, State, Contact person, Phone, Fax
Purchases	P.O.#, Order date, Amount, Vendor#, Employee#
Employee	Employee#, Name, Address, Home phone number, Date hired
Purchase-Inventory	P.O.#, Item#, Unit cost, Quantity purchased, Extension
Purchase-Cash Disbursement	P.O.#, Disbursement voucher#
Inventory	Item#, Description, Quantity on hand
Cash	Bank account#, Bank name, Bank address, Balance
Cash Disbursement	Disbursement voucher#, Check#, Date, Amount

Additional information:

- Quest is a retail company and it often carries new items of inventories.
- Quest would like to include potential vendors in its vendor table.
- Most vendors allow credit purchases.
- Use the same employee table for internal agents.

CHAPTER 3

USING ACCESS *TO IMPLEMENT* A RELATIONAL DATABASE

INTRODUCTION

This chapter introduces the *Microsoft Access* database management system (DBMS) to provide hands-on practice in designing a database. After completing this chapter, you should be able to:

- Understand the *Access* objects, including tables, queries, forms, reports, pages, and macros.
- Create, open and display tables based on the data model.
- Create forms to enter data into tables.
- Establish relationships among tables.

MICROSOFT ACCESS

Most integrated information systems use databases. The software program that defines the database; provides for simplified data entry; manipulates, stores, and retrieves data; and produces reports from the data is called the database management system. *Microsoft Access* (*Access*) is a relational database management system. *Access* refers to the structures and methods used to manage the data as objects. There are four types of objects, which are grouped in the top row of the *Access* database window in Figure 3-1.

Tables are the most important object. As you have already learned, a relational database means that the data is stored in tables or relations. On the surface, a table acts similarly to an Excel table to store/collect data. Thus, the various tables contain *all* the data in a relational database.

Queries allow the user to create questions about the data stored in the database. For example, queries can be used to locate and display a subset of the records of a table (the **select** query), to modify data using one of the **action** queries such as combining information from several tables into a single result, to perform calculations on fields, or to specify criteria for searching the data.

Forms allow the user to see data from tables in another view, usually one record at a time. This often facilitates data entry. Forms can be customized so that they are an exact copy of an existing paper form, making it easier to move from hard copy to soft copy. In a fully automated setting, the form could be filled out on screen at the time of purchase, removing a step, and greatly enhancing the simplicity and accuracy of data entry.

FIGURE 3-1

Reports utilize data created from queries and from one or more tables to provide the user with meaningful information in a printed format. Data can be sorted, grouped, and summarized in almost limitless arrangements in reports. As a result, using reports, you can produce documents such as invoices, purchase orders, sales summaries, and financial statements. However, where the user can enter and edit the data in a Form, you cannot do so with the data in a Report.

The last section, **Macros & Code**, includes **Macros**, which are an advanced *Access* object. **Macros** perform specific, user-specified, automated tasks, such as opening a form, printing a report, or going to the last record. They can also assist in the creation of turnkey applications that anyone can use, whether or not they have experience with *Access*. Another more advanced object in *Access* is the **Module**. **Modules** are similar to **Macros** in that they increase the functionality of the database by allowing the user to write statements and procedures in *Visual Basic* and store them as a unit. These can then either stand alone or be attached to either forms or reports for increased functionality.

REQUIREMENTS

The objective of these assignments is not to provide you with expertise in the development of a database, but to provide you with an initiation to and an appreciation of both the complexity and the power of a database when used to create an accounting information system.

Good programming procedures require a certain amount of structure or standardization. For example, when saving tables, queries, forms, and reports created in a database, it is often useful to use a naming convention (i.e., a method which names the objects in a way that will let the user know to which classification the object belongs). This assists the designer and the user alike in navigating throughout the database. You will notice that we have adopted such a convention in this book.

Please read the following sections carefully. They are intended to be tutorial in nature as well as providing you with the information necessary to complete your *Access* assignments. In some instances, the assignment provides you with explicit instructions about creating necessary tables, forms, queries, and reports. However, in other instances, the assignment allows you to make choices about design considerations such as form style, size, font size, etc. Therefore, it is imperative to follow the directions carefully **AND** to critique the forms and reports you create from a user's perspective. When viewing the final product, user friendliness is critical!

Finally, as is always when you are dealing with technology, it is important to **back your work up frequently**! In the case of *Access*, you do not need to save your database when you close it. It will save automatically. However, you should make a duplicate copy of it and store it on a secondary storage medium.

Creating and Opening a Database

To create a new database in *Access*, you must first launch the *Access* application. When you launch Access, you will notice an **Available Templates** section in the middle of the screen. Below that heading, you will see highlighted a **Blank Database** icon (see Figure 3-2).

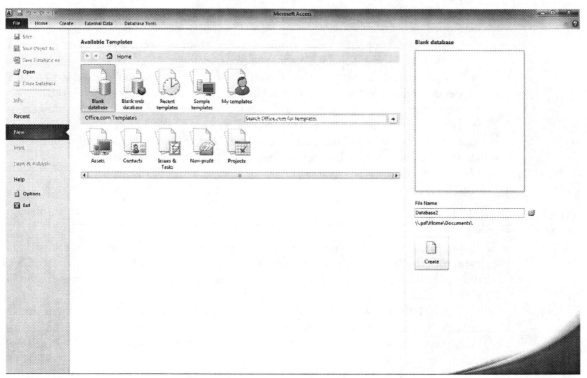

FIGURE 3-2

To the right, you will see a field requesting a **File Name** for the **Blank database**. *Access* has provided a default name for the database. Type over this name and create a database named **Cherokee** (or a name that your instructor has requested). Click the **Create** icon below the File Name field. *Access* will automatically open your new database for you (Figure 3-3).

Creating and Opening a Table

Once your database has been created, it automatically opens a table for you. However, the table has been opened in **Datasheet View**. The **Datasheet View** only allows the designer

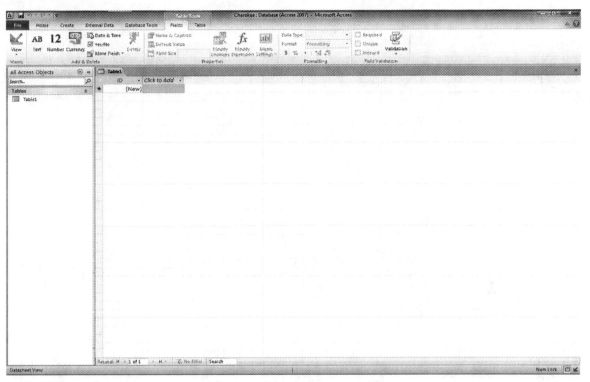

FIGURE 3-3

to see the content of the table and lets *Access* make educated guesses as to the type of data being entered. Since we already know something about the data we are going to enter for Cherokee, we want more control than that, so we will use the **Design View**. The **Design View** provides the designer with the structure of the data, giving the user control over all of the data properties.

1. While in the **Datasheet View**, double-click on the **ID** field to highlight the field, then right-click and select **Rename Field**. Type **CustomerID** in place of **ID**.

2. Now click on the **Home** tab and click on the **View** icon under **Views**. Choose **Design View** . You will be asked to save the table. Name the **Customer Table** and click **OK**.

3. A window appears containing a Table with three columns in the upper pane (**Field Name**, **Data Type**, and **Description**) and **Field Properties** in the lower pane (Figure 3-4).

Field Names can be up to 64 characters and can include almost any combination of letters, numbers, spaces, and special characters (**except** a period, an exclamation point, a backquote character, or brackets because they are reserved Microsoft Visual Basic operators). In addition, obviously a **Field Name** cannot contain leading spaces.

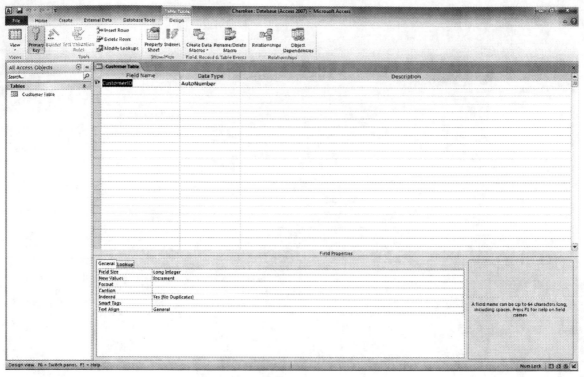

FIGURE 3-4

Although a Field Name can include spaces, spaces in names could produce naming conflicts in Microsoft Visual Basic in some circumstances. Therefore, we will adopt a convention of omitting the spaces in our Field Names and simply capitalizing each new word in the Field Name.

When you tab to the **Data Type** on the Datasheet main menu, you will note a button to pull down a menu. This button allows you to select the **Data Type** for the given New **Field Name**. Take some time to explore the various **Data Types**.

4. We will now complete the **Customer Table** for Cherokee.

In Chapter 2, based on the REA diagram (Figure 2-6), we created the conceptual model of a database for Cherokee. The table structures are as follows:

Inventory Table (<u>Item #</u>, Inventory Description, Inventory Cost, <u>Purchase #</u>, <u>Sale #</u>)

Cash Table (<u>Account #</u>, Account Type, Balance)

Sale Table (<u>Sale #</u>, Sale Date, Sale Amount, Payment Type, <u>Customer ID</u>, <u>Account #</u>)

Purchase Table (<u>Purchase #</u>, Purchase Date, Purchase Amount, <u>Artist ID</u>)

Cash Disbursement Table (<u>Check #</u>, Disbursement Date, Payment Amount,

<u>Artist ID</u>, <u>Account #</u>)

Artist Table	(<u>Artist ID</u>, <u>Artist Name</u>, Artist Address, Artist City, <u>Artist State</u>, Artist ZIP Code, Artist Phone #, Artist Email)
Customer Table	(<u>Customer ID</u>, Customer Name, Customer Address, Customer City, Customer State, Customer ZIP Code, Customer Phone #, Customer Email)

Purchase-Cash Disbursement Table (<u>Purchase #</u>, <u>Check #</u>)

Check the table structure of the **Customer Table**. It has the following attributes: ID, Name, Address, City, State, ZIP Code, Phone #, and Email. We have already created **CustomerID** as the first attribute in the Field Name column. When you create a table, it is very important that you check your work. Before you tab out of the Field Name, make it a habit to check your spelling. Field Names are created when you establish table structures. Everything you do in a database is written in the data dictionary. Therefore, a database can increase in size very quickly. On the practical side, this can create storage issues. Despite the fact that storage has become relatively inexpensive, we know that companies have limited resources. Therefore, it is still important to use storage space efficiently. However, let's assume that storage isn't a problem and you create a Field Name that you later realize you want to change. You can go back and change it but you may want to make sure that it is identical to every other instance in which it appears (i.e., every other table in which you may have used it as a foreign key).

5. Notice that when we changed our **Customer Table** to the **Design View**, the **Primary Key** 🔑 icon appeared beside the **CustomerID** field. The first field name will always default to the **Primary Key** so it is important that we change the field name before we switch to the **Design View**. If **CustomerID** is not marked as the **Primary Key**, make **CustomerID** the **Primary Key** by clicking **Design Tab**, then clicking on the **Primary Key** 🔑 icon in the **Tools** group. Alternatively, you may right-click on the field name and select **Primary Key**.

As we discussed earlier, a primary key is an attribute that uniquely identifies each record. By defining a primary key, Access *does three things:*

- It automatically ensures that no two records in that table will have the same value in the primary key field.
- It keeps records sorted according to the primary key field.
- It speeds up processing.

6. Tab to the **Data Type** column. We are going to assume that Cherokee uses a combination of letters and numbers to identify their customers; therefore, set the data type to **Text** (Figure 3-5). A data type of **Text** can store data consisting of either text or number characters.

You can toggle to the **Field Properties** pane by pressing **F6** or you can move to the **Field Properties** pane by moving your mouse to the desired field. While the **Field Properties** pane may seem intimidating at first, as mentioned previously, this pane allows the designer to specify the structure of each of the fields. In addition, by adjusting the properties, we can specify minimum cardinalities.

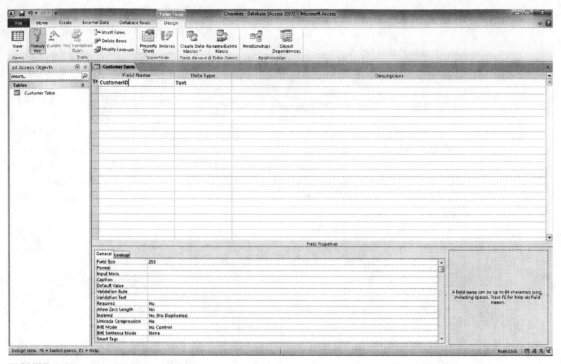

FIGURE 3-5

Data Input Controls

Data input controls deal with the accuracy and completeness of data that are entered into the database. Some of the most important of these are data entry verification controls such as closed-loop verification (discussed later) and edit checks. Edit checks are incorporated into the design of each field to verify and validate the accuracy and/or completeness of data. Table 3-1 describes the most important field properties in *Access*. Most of these can be used as edit checks.

7. Press **F6** to switch to the Field Properties pane of the Table window and set the properties as described in Table 3-2.

8. Note that this is the Primary Key. Therefore, the Required property is set to Yes to ensure that the field will not only be unique, but will also be universal (i.e., not null).

9. The Data Types for all subsequent fields in the **Customer Table** should be set to **Text**. The second Field Name should be **CustomerName**, the Field Size is **45**, and the Caption should be **Customer Name**. The third Field Name should be **CustomerAddress**, the Field Size is **50**, and the Caption should be **Address**. The fourth Field Name should be **CustomerCity** and the field size is **35,** and the Caption should be **City**. (Note that these fields are simplified for purposes of this database. Normally, there would be a separate field for Last Name, First Name, etc.)

Table 3-1

Field Property	Description
Field Size	Sets the maximum size for data stored in a Text, Number or AutoNumber field. In a Text field, the default size is 255 and should be reset to match the field. In Number fields, the default is set to Long Integer.
Format	Specifies how data are to be displayed in a field. Particularly useful in specifying the format for numbers, currency, dates, and times. Note that to look up the appropriate 'string' for the Format property in the Access Help function, you must look under the Input Mask property.
Decimal Places	Specifies the number of digits allowed to the right of the decimal point. Auto allows the Format property to set the decimal places automatically.
Input Mask	Makes data entry easier by adjusting the data entered so that it conforms to the standard set in the Input Mask. Also used to control the values users can enter. Review the Input Mask property help screen to familiarize yourself with this property. See Steps 6–8 below.
Caption	Specifies the text for labels attached to controls created by dragging a field from the field list, and serves as the column heading for the field when seen in Datasheet view. Captions should be descriptive of their Field Names since they will be used as labels in creating Forms and Reports.
Default Value	Specifies a default value for a field (e.g., New York can be set as the Default Value for a City field; the user then has the option of accepting the Default Value or inputting different data).
Validation Rule	Specifies the requirements and limits the values allowed for data entry. For example, the Validation Rule may begin with the word "Like" and continue on with a series of characters placed in quotes to set the requirements for data to be entered into the field. The meaning of these characters is also found under the Input Mask help screen.
Validation Text	The text input in the Validation Text property specifies the message to be displayed to the user when the Validation Rule is violated. For example, when a record is added for a new employee, you can require that the entry in the Start Date field fall between the company's founding date and the current date. If the date entered isn't in this range, you can display the message: "Start date is incorrect."
Required	Specifies whether a value is required in a field; if Yes, the field requires a value, if No, no entry is required. Primary Keys are always required fields. This property is also used to specify whether a record must participate in a relationship (i.e., it is used to specify minimum cardinality participation).
Allow Zero Length	Indicates whether an empty string (i.e., a string containing no characters) is a valid entry; if Yes, the field will accept an empty string even when the Required property is set to Yes.
Indexed	This sets a single-field index (i.e., it speeds the sorting and searching of a table by allowing a speed search on the field). The primary key is always indexed. When a field is indexed, it is also necessary to specify whether duplicates will be allowed. For example, when creating a purchase table, the primary key might be Purchase# and you would not want to allow duplicates. However, when creating a table to add the inventory purchased on a particular purchase, you might still want to be able to sort and search based upon the Purchase# (which would require that field to be indexed), but you would expect that a particular purchase might have several items of inventory. Therefore, duplicates would be allowed.

Table 3-2

Field Size	6
Caption	Customer ID
Validation Rule	Like "???###" (see Table 3-1)
Validation Text	Incorrect Customer ID format. The Customer ID must consist of three letters and 1–3 numbers.
Required	Yes
Indexed	No duplicates

10. The fifth Field Name should be **CustomerState**. The Field Size is **2**. In the Field Properties pane, set the Input Mask property for the **CustomerState** field by typing **>LL** as shown in Figure 3-6. The ">" symbol means that everything that follows will be in uppercase. An "L" symbol means that it must be a letter. Therefore, this input mask will result in any input being changed to two capital letters. For example, if you were to type "ca," *Access* would change the input to "CA" so that it conformed to the standard input for a State abbreviation as required by the input mask. Use an appropriate **Caption** for the **CustomerState** field.

11. The sixth Field Name should be **CustomerZIPCode** (Figure 3-7). The Field Size is **10**. Activate the **Input Mask Wizard** ▣ that appears when you tab into the Input Mask property to aid in making a template for the Zip Code. You will be prompted to save the table first. Click **Yes**.

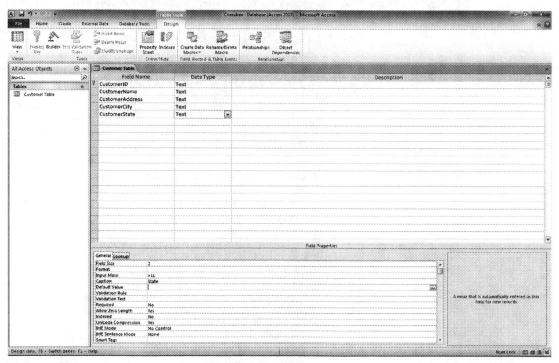

FIGURE 3-6

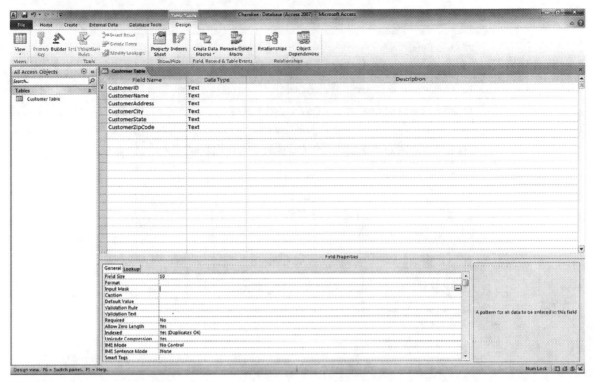

FIGURE 3-7

Select Zip Code from the menu (see Figure 3-8), choose the Zip Code with the hyphen and click **Next** twice. Store the Zip Code with the symbols in the mask. Click on **Next** again and click on **Finish**.

Use an appropriate Caption for this field.

12. The seventh Field Name is **CustomerPhone#**. The Field Size is **14**. The Caption is Customer Telephone Number. Use the Input Mask Wizard to set the Input Mask property to the pre-defined Phone Number setting.

13. The last field is called **CustomerEmail**. The Field Size is **35**; use an appropriate Caption.

14. Congratulations! You are now finished with the table. When you close this object and all objects in the future, use the "X" in the upper right hand corner of the screen to save and close the object.

Now we will create the **Artist Table**.

1. Now that you have created one table in your database, creating additional tables in **Design View** is much easier. Click on the **Create** tab and then click on Tables. Now click on the **Table Design** icon and a new table appears.

2. Create the **Artist Table** in a similar way as you did for the **Customer Table**. The **ArtistID** will be the Primary Key. Its properties should be as described in Table 3-3.

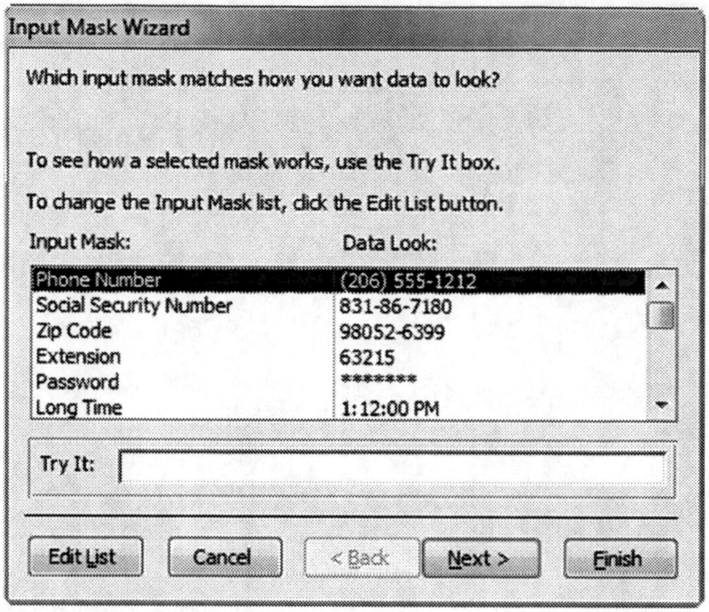

Input Mask Wizard

Which input mask matches how you want data to look?

To see how a selected mask works, use the Try It box.

To change the Input Mask list, click the Edit List button.

Input Mask:	Data Look:
Phone Number	(206) 555-1212
Social Security Number	831-86-7180
Zip Code	98052-6399
Extension	63215
Password	*******
Long Time	1:12:00 PM

Try It:

| Edit List | Cancel | < Back | Next > | Finish |

FIGURE 3-8

Table 3-3

Field Size	6
Caption	Artist ID
Validation Rule	Like "???###"
Validation Text	Incorrect Artist ID format. The Artist ID must consist of three letters and 1–3 numbers.
Required	Yes
Indexed	No duplicates

3. Refer to Cherokee's **Customer Table** structure for the remaining fields in the **Artist Table**. Use field sizes similar to those used in the **Customer Table**.

Completeness Control

Completeness is an important component in internal control. Completeness suggests not only that all data in a transaction are captured, but also that all transactions are recorded. Therefore, it is important to ensure that no documents are lost or misplaced. One way to accomplish this is to prenumber documents and to verify the sequential integrity of the completed documents. We will use this feature in creating the **Purchase Table**.

1. Create a new table in Design view.

2. Refer to Cherokee's table structure for the **Purchase Table**. The first attribute is **Purchase#**. This is the first Field Name. Choose **AutoNumber** as the Data Type. The Caption is **Purchase #**. Make this field the primary key by clicking the **Primary Key** toolbar button.

3. The second Field Name is **PurchaseDate**. The Data type is **Date/Time**. Use the Input Mask Wizard to create the Input Mask property. When prompted to save the table, save it as **Purchase Table**. Choose **Short Date** for the Input Mask as shown in Figure 3-9.

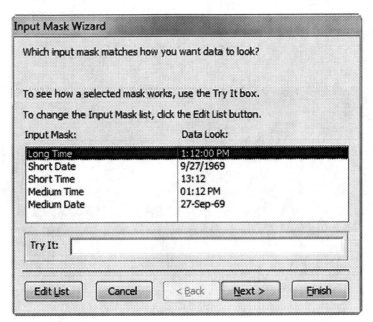

FIGURE 3-9

Click on **Next** twice and then click on **Finish**. After you tab out of the Input Mask property, it should look like this: **99/99/00;0;_**. The Caption is **Purchase Date**.

4. The third Field Name is **PurchaseAmount**. The Data Type is **Currency**. The Caption is **Purchase Amount**.

5. The fourth Field Name is **ArtistID**. The Data Type is **Text**. The field size is **6**. The Caption is **Artist ID**.

*Notice that you have already used the Field Name **ArtistID**. It is the primary key in the **Artist Table**. As we mentioned before, when a field name appears in one table that is a primary key in another table, it is called a **Foreign Key**. Foreign keys are used to link tables together. A foreign key must be the same data type as the corresponding primary key it will be linked to.*

6. You will now save the table as **Purchase Table**.

Creating and Opening a Form

Although the data can be entered from the datasheet view of a table, the utilization of forms makes data easier to enter and makes the database much more user-friendly. A form can display data in almost any format. A very simple form can be designed to display one record at a time. More complex forms can be created as 'fill-in-the-blanks' forms resembling the paper forms a company already uses.

1. We will begin by creating a very simple form. The form for the **Customer Table** will utilize all of the fields we created in this table. Therefore, we really don't have to customize the fields in order to create this form. Highlight the **Customer Table** on the left-hand side of the database window (Figure 3-10). Click on the **Form** icon in **Forms** section of the **Create** tab.

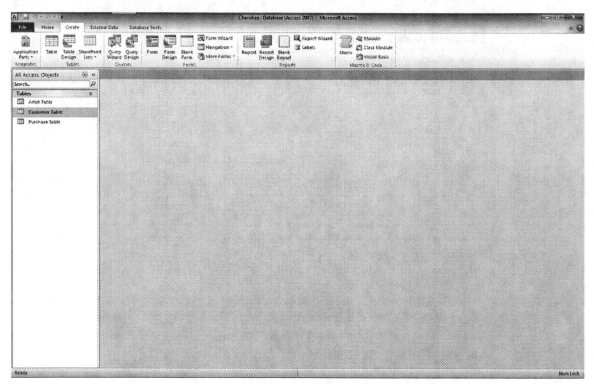

FIGURE 3-10

2. A completed **Customer Form** appears with all the fields that we created in the **Customer Table** (Figure 3-11).

3. However, as you will note, the title of the form appears as "Customer Table." We will change that by double-clicking on the word "Table" and changing it to "Form" (Figure 3-12).

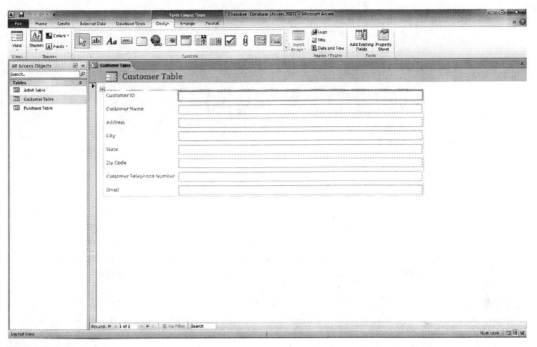

FIGURE 3-11

FIGURE 3-12

4. When you close this form by clicking the **X** in the upper right-hand corner of the form window, you will be prompted to save it. Rename it and save it as **Customer Form** as indicated in Figure 3-13.

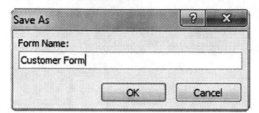

FIGURE 3-13

5. Notice now that Customer Form appears in a new **Forms** section below in the **Tables** section on the left-hand side of your database screen (Figure 3-14).

FIGURE 3-14

6. Open the form again by double-clicking it and enter the information contained in Figure 3-15.

Customer ID	Customer Name	Address	City	State	Zip Code	Customer Telephone Number	Email
BRY067	Mary Bryan	7561 E Larkspur	Scottsdale	AZ	85260-	(480) 555-8823	edwardsgirl@ips.com
EDW075	Frank Edwards	4025 N. Parkway Avenue	Scottsdale	AZ	85251-	(480) 555-1956	iceman@ips.com
SAW055	Margaret Sawyer	22 Goldsmith Avenue	Coral Springs	FL	33071-	(954) 555-8529	knights@ips.com
TET056	Mimi Tetro	24 Winchester Lane	Elwood	NY	11746-	(516) 555-9583	harmon@ips.com

FIGURE 3-15

7. Another relatively easy way to make a form is to use the **Blank Form** icon found in the **Forms** section under the **Create** tab. We will use this method to create the **Artist Table**. Click on **Blank Form** now. In Figure 3-16, you will see a blank form window in the center and a Field List window on the right-hand side listing the three tables that you have created.

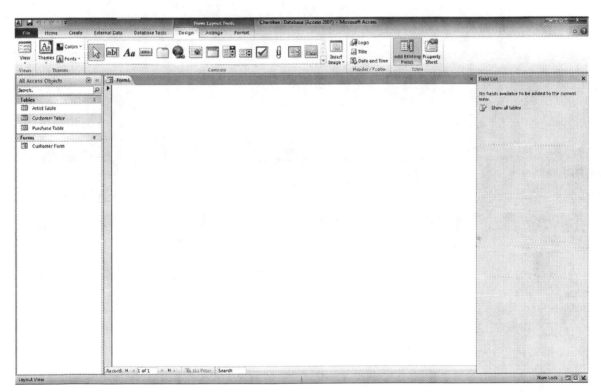

FIGURE 3-16

8. In the **Field List** window on the right, click on **Show all tables** and expand the Artist Table.

9. Notice that all the fields from the **Artist Table** are now visible. Double-click each field to add the fields to the form window (Figure 3-17). Close the Field List window.

10. The form pictured in Figure 3-18 is in **Form View**. As you can see, it needs some adjustments. We need to add a title to this form and we need to make all the captions visible. To do that, we need to switch the form to **Design View**. Click on the **View** icon in the **Views** section.

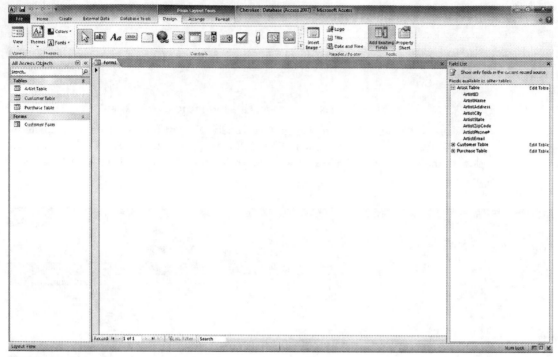

FIGURE 3-17

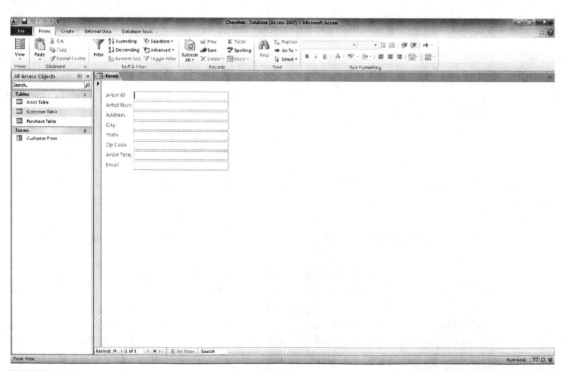

FIGURE 3-18

11. Stretch the form to the right to make more room. Highlight the Captions only and hover your cursor along the right edge until you see a double arrow appear. Stretch the Captions to the right until all of the Captions for all fields are visible (Figure 3-19).

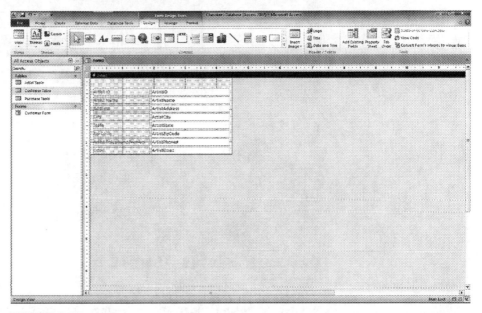

FIGURE 3-19

12. Right-click anywhere on the form and click on **Form Header/Footer**. A header area will appear above the **Detail** area that contains the fields that we added in Step 9 and a footer area appears below (Figure 3-20).

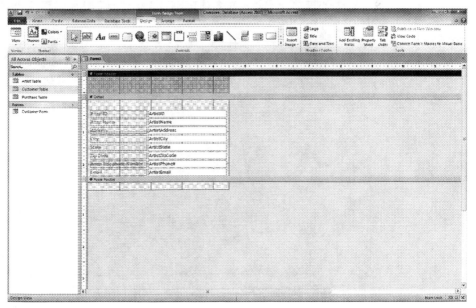

FIGURE 3-20

13. We don't need the footer area, so place your cursor at the bottom of the design grid below the footer and drag the design grid up to the Form Footer bar (Figure 3-21).

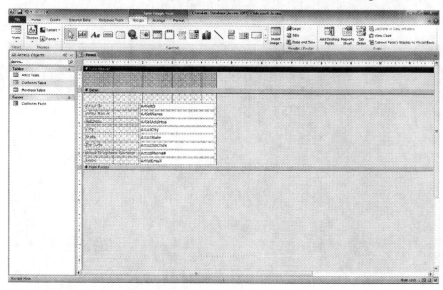

FIGURE 3-21

14. Enlarge the **Form Header** area by placing your cursor just above the **Detail** bar and dragging it down. Click the **Label** *Aa* icon in the **Controls** section of the **Design** tab. Drag a rectangle out in **Form Header** area and enter "Artist Form" in this rectangle. Format the label by clicking on the **Format** tab, highlighting the text and using a **bold**, size **18 font** (see Figure 3-22).

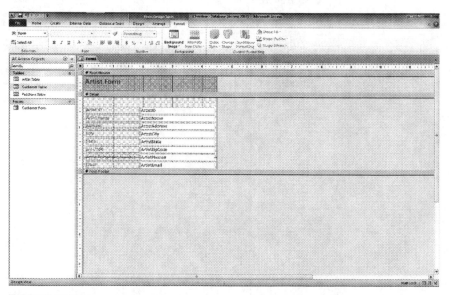

FIGURE 3-22

15. Close the form and save it as **Artist Form** when asked. Your **Artist Form** is now listed in the database.

16. Open the **Artist Form** again by double-clicking on the **Artist Form** in the **Form View**. As we mentioned earlier, it is important to pay attention to user-friendliness. The size and captions of the fields are part of this. Notice that the **Artist Telephone Number** label is much longer than the rest of the labels. The same problem occurred when we created the **Customer Form**. We can correct this problem by clicking on **Views** and selecting **Design View** . Note that you can toggle back and forth between the **Design View** and the **Form View** as much as is needed to adjust your form and make sure it is user-friendly.

Since the caption for the artist's telephone number is too long, change it from **Artist Telephone Number** to **Phone #**. Click back to the **Form View**. Notice that now the labels are all approximately the same size.

17. We can also adjust the spacing between the **Labels** and the **Text Boxes**. A **Text Box** is the area in which data is viewed or edited on forms and reports. Therefore, this is the area in which the data is entered into a form, which then goes into the table.

18. Click on one of the **Labels** to highlight it. It doesn't matter which label you click on. Place your cursor on the right edge of the label so that it appears as a double arrow. As you drag the label to the left, notice that you are changing the size of all the labels. Adjust the size of the **Labels** so that you see the text of all the labels clearly but there isn't a great amount of blank space after the text. Toggle back to the **Form View** to see how your form appears to you now. Once you are satisfied, close the **Artist Form**. You do not need to enter any data into this form (Figure 3-23).

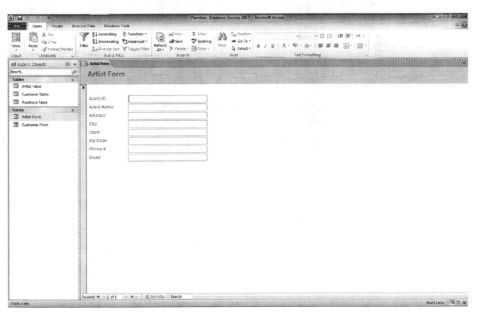

FIGURE 3-23

Creating Relationships to Link Tables

As stated previously, *Access* is a relational database. This implies that associations or relationships are created between attributes (columns) in two tables to link the data from one table to another. This is important because the relations allow the data to be brought together in forms and for reporting purposes. Thus, as a result of the relations we build into the database, we can very easily and quickly query the database to discover what customer purchased a particular piece of artwork. The REA model of Cherokee's expenditure cycle is reproduced in Figure 3-24 for a review.

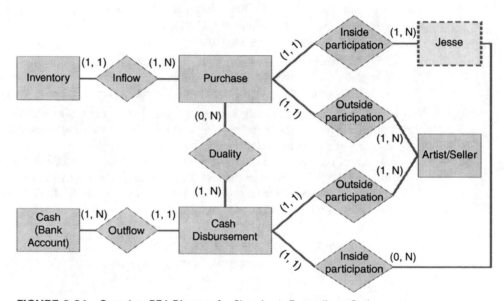

FIGURE 3-24 Complete REA Diagram for Cherokee's Expenditure Cycle

Since each of the artist's pieces can be purchased in any number of purchase events, there should be a one-to-many relationship established between the **Artist Table** and the **Purchase Table** so that data regarding artists does not have to be duplicated on the **Purchase Table**. Notice that in *Access*, only the maximum cardinality is shown in the relationship window.

In this section, you will set up these other tables for Cherokee and create relationships among them. The following instructions will aid in setting up a relationship linking the **Purchase Table** to the **Artist Table**.

1. From the **Relationships** section in the **Database Tools** tab, click on the **Relationships** icon. A **Show Table** window pops up listing the three tables that you have created (Figure 3-25).

2. Add both the **Purchase Table** and the **Artist Table** as shown in Figure 3-26. Close the **Show Table** dialogue box.

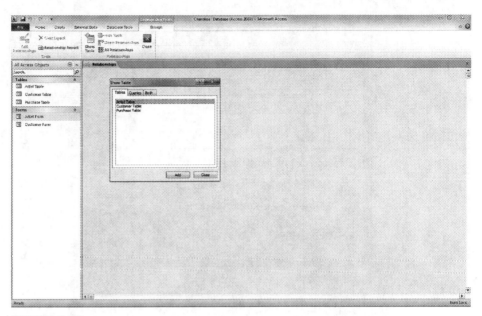

FIGURE 3-25

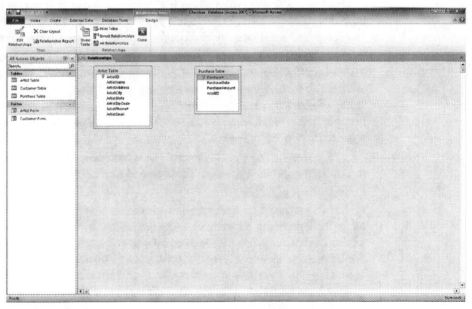

FIGURE 3-26

Click and drag the **ArtistID** field in the **Artist Table** to the **ArtistID** field in the **Purchase Table**.

3. The **Edit Relationships** window pops up. From this window, click on the **Enforce Referential Integrity** check box as indicated in Figure 3-27. Referential integrity ensures that

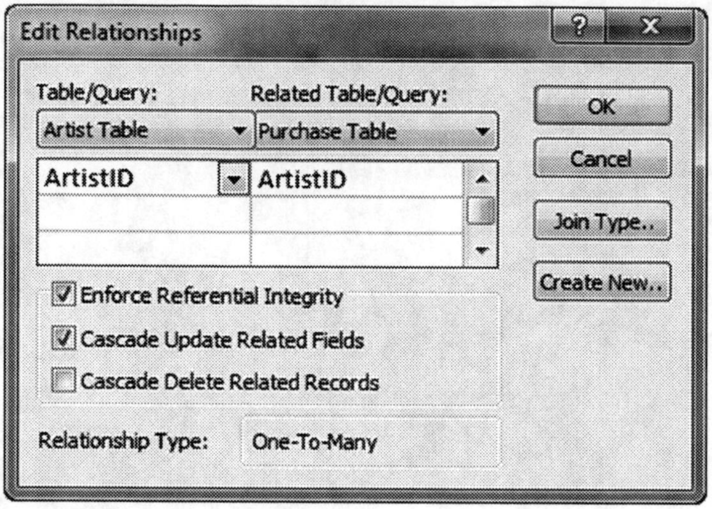

FIGURE 3-27

records referenced by a primary key cannot be deleted unless all records containing the foreign key are first removed. Thus, in this case, an artist now cannot be deleted if there is a related purchase and you cannot delete an artist from the **Purchase Table** screen. In addition, enforcing referential integrity also checks to make sure that the two fields' data types match.

4. Check the **Cascade Update Related Fields** box. This will result in updating the values of all related foreign keys if the value of a primary key is changed. For example, if an ArtistID is changed for one of the artists in the Artist Table, the ArtistID in the Purchase Table will be automatically updated for every purchase related to that artist so that the relationship between artist and purchase will not be broken. This cascade update effect occurs without displaying any message.

5. Click on the **Create** button. The relationship has now been created between the **Artist Table** and the **Purchase Table** (see Figure 3-28).

6. Save and close.

In this chapter, you learned how to construct tables and relationships in *Access* based on an REA diagram. As we have discussed, tables are the fundamental storage entity for a relational database. You also learned how to construct forms from the tables you created. Forms provide an alternative way for the user to enter data, making it easy to both enter and change the information contained in a table. In the following chapters, we will explore more advanced forms. We will also create queries and reports while we construct the Sales/Collection cycle, the Acquisition/Payment cycle, and the Human Resource cycle.

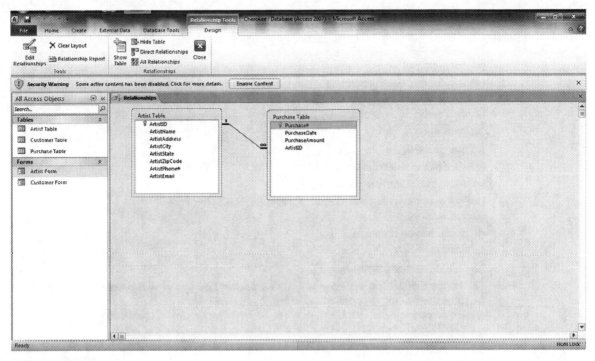

FIGURE 3-28

KEY TERMS

tables	reports	validation rule
queries	referential integrity	input mask
forms	completeness Control	

QUESTIONS AND PROBLEMS FOR REVIEW

3.1 Which of the following are the objects in *Access*?

(a) Tables

(b) Forms

(c) Reports

(d) Queries

(e) All of the above.

3.2 In *Access*, we use tables in a database for
    (a) data entry.
    (b) data storage.
    (c) data retrieval.
    (d) Two of the above are correct.

3.3 In *Access*, we use forms in a database for
    (a) data entry.
    (b) data storage.
    (c) data retrieval.
    (d) Two of the above are correct
    (e) None of the above is correct.

3.4 One important completeness control discussed in the chapter is the
    (a) data control.
    (b) prenumbered documents.
    (c) filled-in forms.
    (d) All of the above are correct.

3.5 The feature that ensures that records that are referenced by a foreign key cannot be deleted unless the record containing the primary key is first removed is called
    (a) entity integrity.
    (b) key integrity.
    (c) referential integrity.
    (d) record integrity.

PROBLEMS

3.1 Cherokee Art and Antique Store—Tables and Relationships
You have already created the Purchase Table, Artist Table, and Customer Table. Review the REA diagram in Figure 3-24 and now create the remaining tables and relationships for Cherokee's Acquisition/Payment cycle using the table structure that was previously established and is provided for you once more below.

Inventory Table (Item #, Inventory Description, Inventory Cost, Purchase #, Sale #)
Cash Table (Account #, Account Type, Balance)
Sale Table (Sale #, Sale Date, Sale Amount, Payment Type, Customer ID, Account #)
Purchase Table (Purchase #, Purchase Date, Purchase Amount, Artist ID)
Cash Disbursement Table (Check #, Disbursement Date, Payment Amount, Artist ID, Account #)
Artist Table (Artist ID, Artist Name, Artist Address, Artist City, Artist State, Artist ZIP Code, Artist Phone #, Artist Email)
Customer Table (Customer ID, Customer Name, Customer Address, Customer City, Customer State, Customer ZIP Code, Customer Phone #, Customer Email)
Purchase-Cash Disbursement Table (Purchase #, Check #)

3.2 Cherokee Art and Antique Store–Forms
Create a form for Cherokee to enter data into the Inventory Table. You do not need to enter any Inventory into this form at this time.

CHAPTER 4

SALES/COLLECTION BUSINESS PROCESS

INTRODUCTION

In the previous chapter, we looked at a very simple revenue cycle for Cherokee Art and Antique Store. In this chapter, we will look at a much more complex business process. A *business process* is basically synonymous with a transaction cycle. The Sales/Collection business process is often referred to as the revenue transaction cycle. The Sales/Collection process includes the instigation events (such as marketing events, i.e., sales calls, advertising campaigns, etc.), the mutual commitment events (i.e., customer orders), the economic decrement events (i.e., the sale and shipment), and the economic increment event (i.e., the cash receipt). We might also see an economic decrement reversal event (i.e., sales returns and allowances).

To model the Sales/Collection business process in a database, it will be useful to create more complex forms and we will need to create queries. After completing this chapter, you should be able to use Microsoft *Access* to:

- Create queries involving single tables.
- Create queries involving simple calculations.
- Create queries involving more than one table.
- Create queries involving simple criteria.
- Create forms with subforms from tables.
- Create combo boxes in a form.
- Create a simple report based on a query.

SALES/COLLECTION PROCESS OVERVIEW

Basic Concepts and Definitions

As we illustrated in Figure 1-3, the revenue cycle interfaces with the conversion cycle, the financing cycle, and the financial reporting system. The financial reporting system interfaces with all of the cycles.

Extending this to the framework of business processes, we can see that goods and services are made available to a company's Sales/Collection process as a result of the Conversion, Acquisition/Payment and Payroll processes. The Sales/Collection process turns those goods and services into cash, which is made available to the Financing process.

For this to happen, the Sales/Collection process must include at least one economic event that transfers out the goods and services (i.e., a decrement event) and at least one economic event that transfers in the cash (i.e., an increment event). The Sales/Collection process for all firms is similar regardless of whether the firm is engaged in manufacturing, in service, or in retail.

Labor is typically not tracked and matched to the revenue-generating activity since labor costs are normally aggregated into a selling, general, and administrative expense and accumulated in the payroll cycle. One exception to this is in the case of service providers, where labor takes the place of inventory. Other exceptions include companies that use delivery services.

Tragg's Custom Surfboards

Background Tragg's Custom Surfboards is located at 8713 Montauk Drive, La Selva Beach, CA 95076. Their telephone number is (831) 555-1513; their fax number is (831) 555-1613. Tragg's Custom Surfboards both manufactures and sells surfboards and surfing equipment. Dan Tragg began shaping, designing, and manufacturing his own surfboards 25 years ago. He soon discovered that there was a demand for them among his friends and acquaintances. He started selling them casually and ultimately founded the business in 1988. Initially, his boards were sold through a few select dealers. As demand grew, however, he set up a website and opened his own store. The store now carries a stock of surfboards and Dan continues to fill custom orders.

Model the Revenue Cycle using REA As we did in Chapter 1 for Cherokee Art and Antique Store, we need to model the revenue cycle using the REA topology[1]. Since all sales are final, we will collapse the custom order event into the sales event to keep things simple for the company.

Sales begin with the customer coming into the store or can commence with an e-mail order or a telephone order from the customer. Tragg's requires a 50% deposit before beginning a custom order and this deposit is non-refundable. Custom orders usually take 4-5 weeks to complete.

Whether a custom order or a sale from stock, the customer has a choice between four basic board styles: Egotist, Imposer, Nice Devil, or King Creator. The customer can also choose between two fins: single fin or glassed-on fin. Coloring is offered in opaque or transparent. The customer can choose his or her own pigment for the board by sending in a color chip obtained from the paint section of their local hardware store.

Pricing is largely dependent upon the length of the board plus any extra features that are requested. For example, a board up to 6'11" begins at $475. Anything longer than that goes up $25 in price for every six inches requested. All boards come with certain standard features, depending upon the board style chosen. In addition, the customer can add *only*

---

[1]Tragg's Custom Surfboards has more than just the economic increment and decrement events occurring. We now also have an instigation event in which Dan Tragg markets the surfboards and surfing equipments on the web. This website also generates inquiries from potential customers. As stated, there is a mutual commitment event (i.e., the custom orders) that is collapsed into the sales event. In addition, for simplicity's sake, we have chosen not to model the instigation event. Rather, we begin with the sales event.

one of the following custom stripes to his or her surfboard: a pinline stripe for $20, a colored competition stripe for $40, color lamination (tint or opaque) for $40, cloth design for $50, airbrush finish for $25, a gloss and polish for $45, or an extra 10-oz. volan glass layer for $25. (We realize that, in reality, customers might well order more than one of these custom extras. However, we have limited it to one custom extra per order for simplicity's sake.) Tragg's stores the information on extra features and details on other inventories in a separate table.

When orders come in (custom orders or otherwise), a Sales Invoice form is completed. All sales are final; there are no returns allowed. As a result, the sales order is the sales invoice. (Again to simplify this example, we will assume that no sales tax is charged. In reality, sales tax would be charged on all in-store sales and internet sales made to California residents.)

Customers must arrange to pick up the surfboards in the store or have them shipped. Final payment is due when the surfboard is picked up or before it is shipped. In addition, some customers may pay for several transactions at once (i.e., write one check for several invoices).

Although Tragg's maintains several bank accounts (one general checking account, one payroll account, and one savings account), most of the cash receipts and cash disbursements are handled through the general checking account. Most cash receipts come from sales; however, Tragg's does have a few investments that result in dividend income and are deposited in the general checking account.

According to the descriptions of Tragg's business processes in the revenue cycle, Figure 4-1 is an REA diagram created to model the business activities for Tragg's.

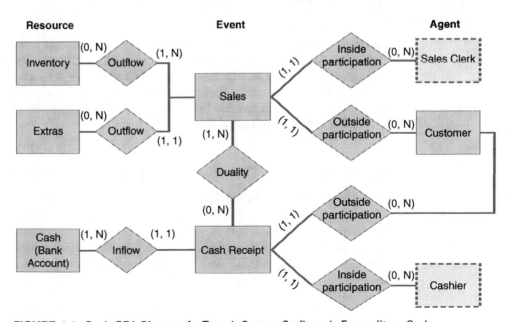

FIGURE 4-1 Basic REA Diagram for Tragg's Custom Surfboards Expenditure Cycle

Create a Relational Database for Tragg's Following the REA Diagram
To start with a relatively simple design of a database, we will not create tables for those entities in dotted lines in Figure 4-1. In addition, as noted in the model, the relationship between
the entities Sales and Inventory is many-to-many. This is because it is possible that we will
have several of one particular kind, size, and color surfboard in stock at one time. Therefore,
as you learned in Chapter 2, we cannot use a foreign key link to join these entities. You must
create a separate table to represent each many-to-many relationship. Keep in mind that we
have limited customers to one Extra on their surfboard. Therefore, the relationship between
Extras and Sales is a one-to-many relationship and no separate table is necessary.

Accordingly, Tragg's table structure for the Sales/Collection Business Process can
be represented as follows:

Cash Table (<u>CashAcctNo</u>, AcctType)

Inventory Table (<u>InventoryID</u>, InventoryDescription, InventoryCost, InventoryPrice)

Extras Table (<u>ExtrasID</u>, ExtrasDescription, ExtrasCost, ExtrasPrice)

Cash Receipt Sale Table (<u>CashReceiptID</u>, <u>InvoiceNo</u>, AmountApplied)

Sales Inventory Table (InvoiceNo, InventoryID, QuantityOrdered, <u>ExtrasID</u>)

Cash Receipt Table (CashReceiptID, CRData, CustomerCheckNo,
<u>CustomerID, CashAcctNo</u>)

Sales Table (<u>InvoiceNo</u>, InvoiceDate, <u>ExtrasID</u>, <u>CustomerID</u>)

Customer Table (<u>CustomerID</u>, CustomerLastName, CustomerFirstName,
CustomerAddress1, CustomerAddress2, CustomerCity, CustomerState,
CustomerZip, CustomerPhone)

Creating Tragg's Relational Database using Access Open the Chapter 4
database for Tragg's Custom Surfboards that came with your book. *You must download
this database and save it to your hard drive in order to use it for your assignment.* Note
that all the tables, some relationships, and some forms have already been created for the
Sales/Collection Business Process. Take some time to examine the tables, forms, and the
relationships that have been created thus far.

The Sales Form: Creating a Form with a Subform

Creating a **Sales Form** is a more complex task than creating the forms we have worked with
in Chapter 2. The **Sales Form** is the Sales Order for Tragg's. Therefore, it must be able to
obtain information about customers, inventory, and extras. The database that we have provided for you has partial data in it so that you can now complete a sale. If you have not yet
done so, download and open the Tragg's Custom Surfboard database and take some time to
acquaint yourself with the **Customer Table**, **Inventory Table**, and the **Extras Table**.

In addition, since the creation of the **Sales Form** will result in entering data into both
the **Sales Table** and the **Sales Inventory Table**, we will need to establish the necessary
relationships between these tables, before creating the **Sales Form**.

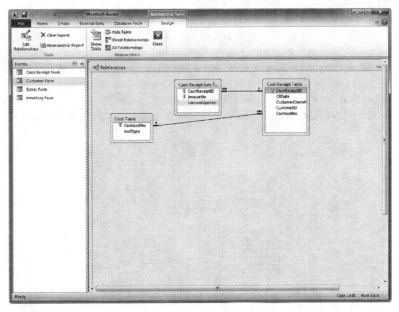

FIGURE 4-2

1. Click on the **Relationships** icon in the **Relationships** section of the **Database Tools** tab to open the Relationships window (Figure 4-2).

2. Click on **Show Table** in the **Relationships** section of the **Design** tab.

3. Hold down the **Ctrl** key and click on the **Customer Table**, the **Extras Table**, the **Inventory Table**, the **Sales Inventory Table**, and the **Sales Table** (Figure 4-3).

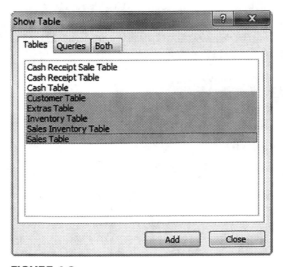

FIGURE 4-3

4. Click **Add**. Then click **Close**.

5. Look at the arrangement of the tables as they have been added to the Relationship window. *Access* randomly places them in the window (Figure 4-4). However, for the sake of an orderly AIS design, it is useful for us to think about Resources, Events, and Agents (i.e., the REA diagram). Drag the tables so that they are generally placed in the same locations that they would appear if you had created an REA diagram. This will be helpful to you in the event that you need to locate a table in the Relationship window later.

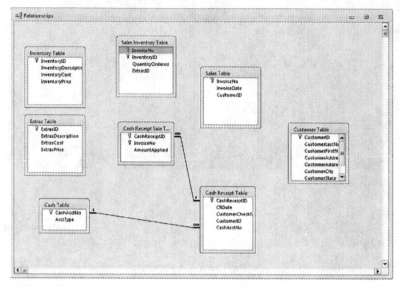

FIGURE 4-4

6. Create the necessary relationships by linking the primary keys to their foreign keys in the appropriate tables. For example, drag **CustomerID** from the **Customer Table** to **CustomerID** in the **Sales Table**. When you do this, the **Edit Relationships** window appears; check the **Enforce Referential Integrity** and the **Cascade Update Related Fields** buttons and click **Create** (Figure 4-5).

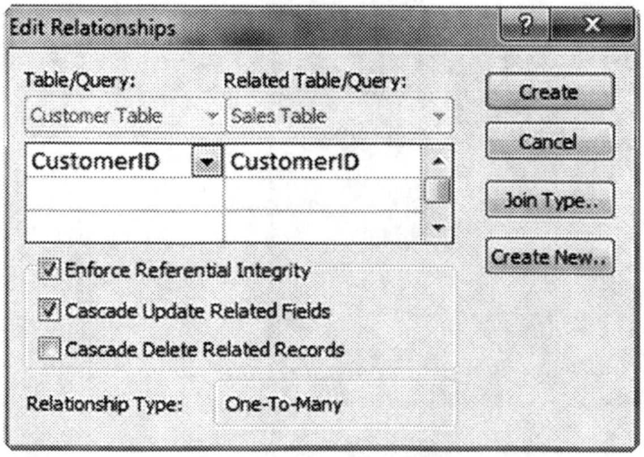

FIGURE 4-5

7. Create all the remaining relationships.

8. Close the Relationships window.

Now that the Relationships have been created, we are ready to begin creating the **Sales Form**.

9. Click on the **Form Wizard** ![Form Wizard] icon in the **Forms** section of the **Create** tab.

10. From the Tables/Queries pull-down menu, select the **Sales Table** and select all three fields for inclusion in the form (Figure 4-6).

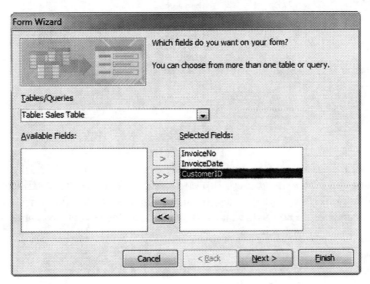

FIGURE 4-6

11. Select the **Customer Table** and select all the fields for inclusion in the form.

NOTE: Before you select fields for inclusion from this table and from tables in the future, it is helpful to make sure that the last field is highlighted in the Selected Fields window. If it is not, the fields may be out of order when the form is created and you might have to rearrange them!

12. Remember that in some cases a field represents a foreign key (i.e., it is a primary key in another table) and, therefore, provides the relationship between tables. Therefore, it is important that we select the field from the correct table for inclusion in the form. The **CustomerID** is one of these fields. It is represented in both the **Sales Table** and the **Customer Table**. We do not want to include both fields in the form, so the question arises as to which field should be included in the **Sales Form**. Since this is the **Sales Form**, the **CustomerID** field included should be the one from the **Sales Table**.

In addition, there is no need to include the **CustomerPhone** field in the **Sales Form**. Return the **CustomerTable.CustomerID** and the **CustomerPhone** fields back in the Available Fields window by selecting each field individually and clicking on the **Left Arrow** ![<] icon (Figure 4-7).

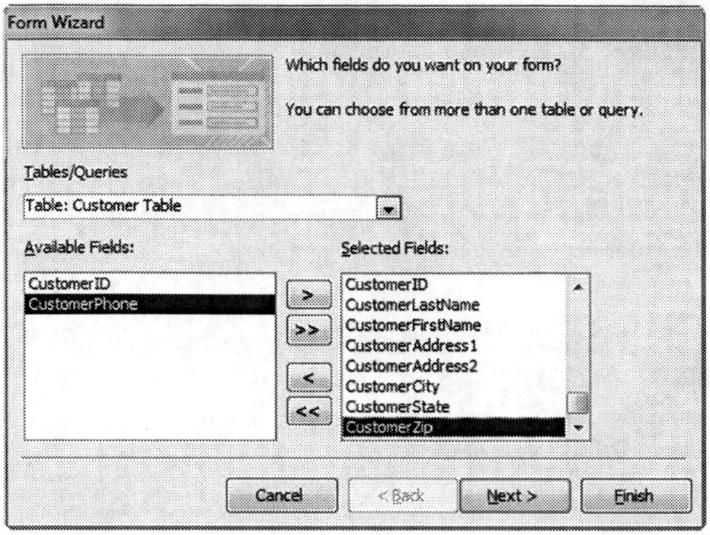

FIGURE 4-7

13. Select the **Sales Inventory Table** and, as before, select all fields for inclusion. Return the **Sales Inventory Table.InvoiceNo** field to the Available Fields window (Figure 4-8). We have already included the **InvoiceNo** field from the **Sales Table**. Therefore, we do not include it again from the **Sales Inventory Table**.

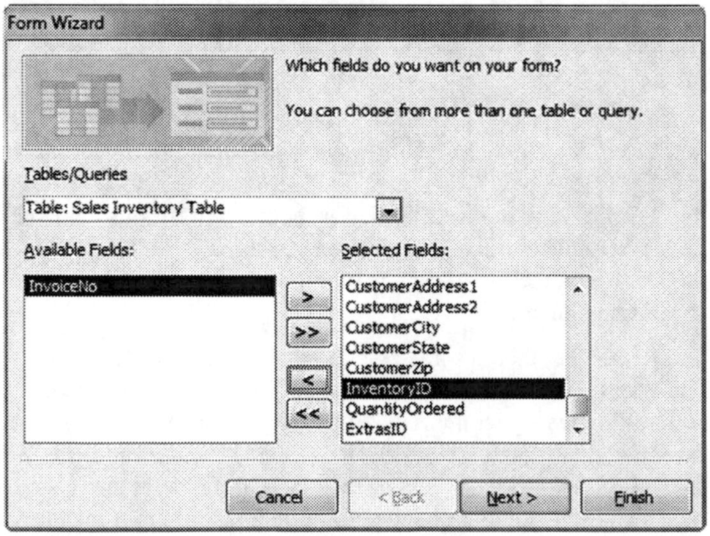

FIGURE 4-8

14. Select **Inventory Table** and then select **InventoryDescription** and **Inventory-Price** for inclusion in the form. Note that you do not need the **InventoryID** field included in the form because you have already included this field when you added it from the **Sales Inventory Table** (Figure 4-9).

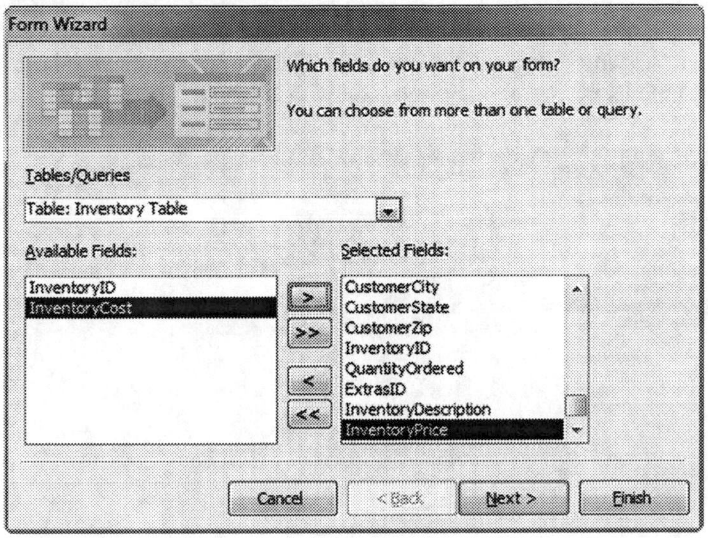

FIGURE 4-9

15. Select the **Extras Table** and select **ExtrasDescription** and **ExtrasPrice** for inclusion in the form (Figure 4-10). You do not need the **ExtrasID** field included in the form because you included the **ExtrasID** field when you added the **Sales Inventory Table**.

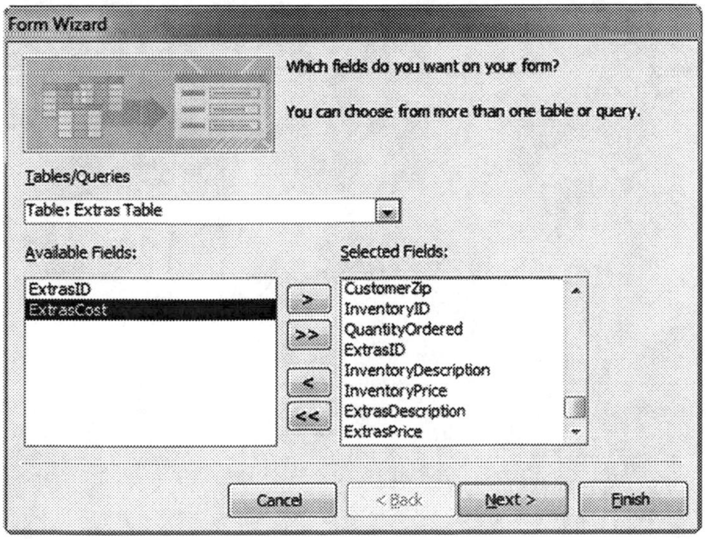

FIGURE 4-10

16. Click the **Next** button. The Form Wizard (Figure 4-11) automatically suggests a layout for the **Sales Form** (containing fields from the **Sales Table** and the **Customer Table**) with a subform (containing the fields from the **Sales Inventory Table**, the **Inventory Table** and the **Extras Table**). Note that, if the Form Wizard does not suggest this layout, one likely explanation is that you have not created the appropriate relationships between the tables required for this form. If this occurs, you should go back and examine your relationships before continuing on with this step.

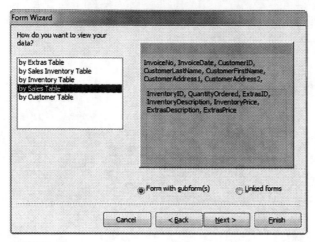

FIGURE 4-11

Accept the layout by clicking the **Next** button.

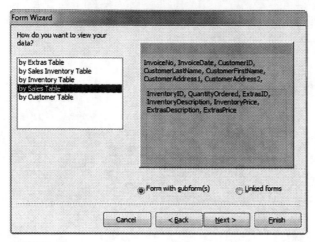

FIGURE 4-12

17. Select the Tabular layout for the subform in the next window (Figure 4-12) and click **Next**.

18. Select a style for your form and click **Next**. Change the name of the form to **Sales Form** (leave the name of the subform alone). Click on **Modify the form's design**. Click on **Finish** (Figure 4-13).

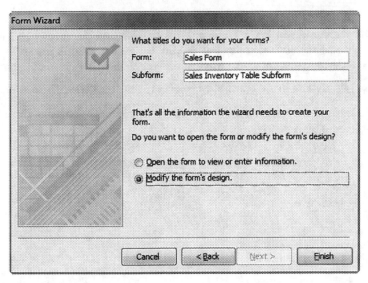

FIGURE 4-13

19. We will now make substantial adjustments to the form's design (Figure 4-14).

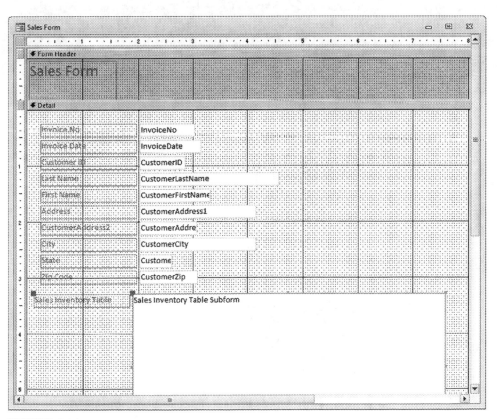

FIGURE 4-14

20. Shrink the Navigation Pane containing the database objects on the left-hand side of the database window by clicking on the left double arrow « at the top of the Navigation Pane so that we can work with the Sales Form in the full window. Note that you will be able to retrieve the Navigation Pane at any time by clicking on the right double arrow » . Switch to the Form View by clicking on the **View** icon in the **Views** section of the **Design** tab. Notice that the city, state, and zip code portion of the address are on separate lines (Figure 4-15).

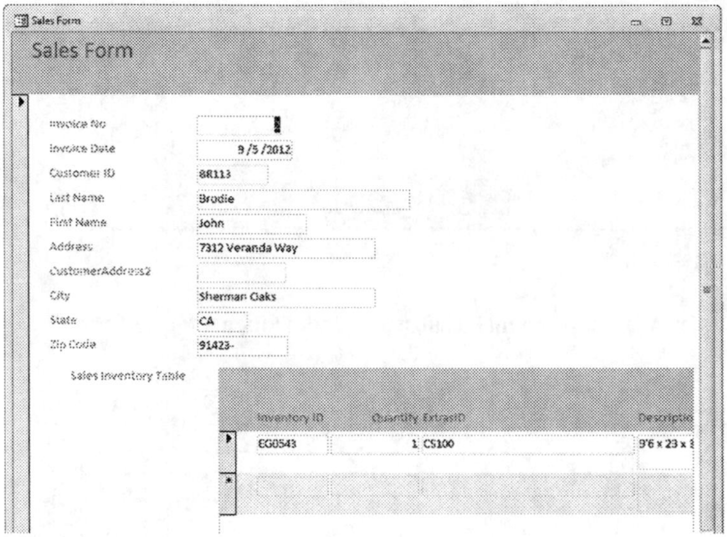

![Sales Form window showing fields: Invoice No, Invoice Date 9/5/2012, Customer ID 8R113, Last Name Brodie, First Name John, Address 7312 Veranda Way, CustomerAddress2, City Sherman Oaks, State CA, Zip Code 91423-, Sales Inventory Table with Inventory ID EG0543, Quantity 1, ExtraID CS100, Description 9'6 x 23 x]

FIGURE 4-15

Since this information will be returned automatically by the database once the **CustomerID** has been entered, we can consolidate the information and make the form more user-friendly.

21. Return to the Design View and left click on the Form Selector (the square in the upper left corner of the form where the two rulers meet). A black square will appear (Figure 4-16).

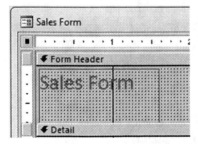

FIGURE 4-16

22. Now right click the black square and select **Properties** in the pull-down menu. The Property Sheet window appears on the right-hand side of the screen (Figure 4-17).

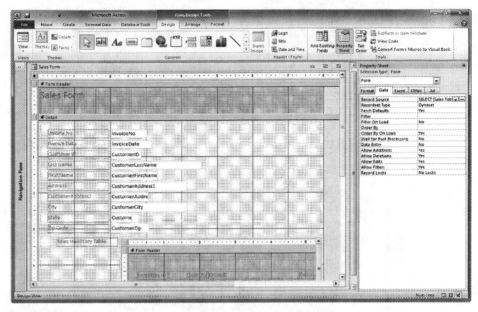

FIGURE 4-17

23. Click on the **Data** tab in the **Property Sheet**. Then double-click on the **Build** button next to the **Record Source** property. This opens Query Builder window (Figure 4-18). Notice that the **Sales Table** and the **Customer Table** appear at the top pane of the window linked by **CustomerID**. Also notice that all of the fields that we added to the form appear in the columns in the lower pane of the window, called the *design grid*. Close the **Property Sheet**.

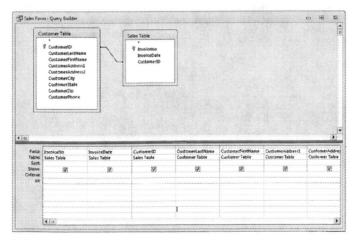

FIGURE 4-18

24. Click on the **Sort** property under the **InvoiceNo** field. Using the pull-down menu, select **Ascending** for this property so that the Sales Invoices will sort according to Invoice No (Figure 4-19).

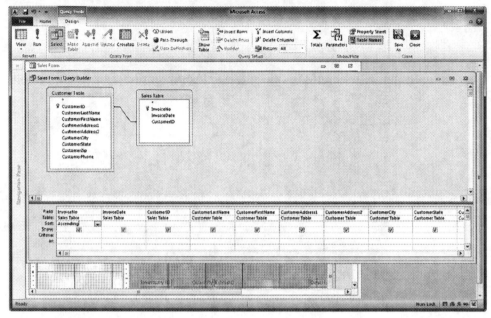

FIGURE 4-19

25. Scroll to the right of the design grid until you reach an open column (the column after **CustomerZip**). Click in the Field cell of this column and click on the **Builder** ⚛ Builder icon. This opens the **Expression Builder** window, which facilitates the creation of new fields in a query (Figure 4-20).

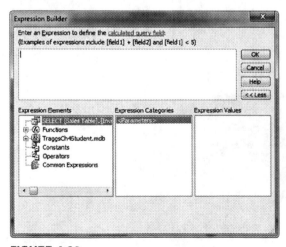

FIGURE 4-20

26. Click on the database in the far left lower window, click on Tables and then select the **Customer Table** (Figure 4-21).

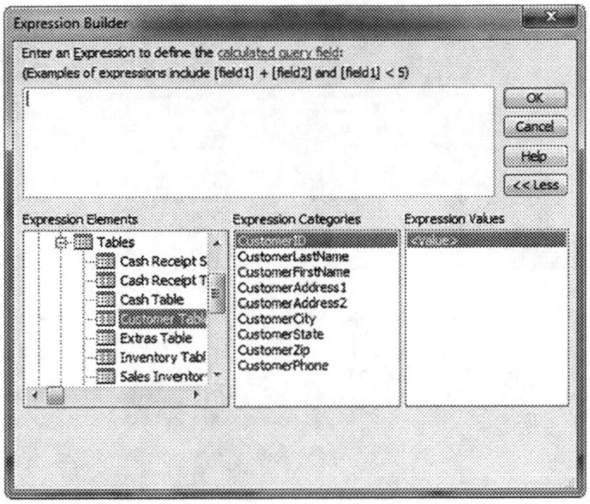

FIGURE 4-21

27. We are going to create a composite address field for the customer's city, state, and zip code so that all three fields are combined into one field, in a format similar to what you would see in a mailing label (Figure 4-22). Type **CustomerCompAddress:** in the upper portion of the Expression Builder window. Double-click on **CustomerCity**; click on **&**, type **", "** (typed as an open quotation, comma, space, close quotation). Click on **&** and double-click on **CustomerState**. Click on **&** and type **" "** (typed as an open quotation, three spaces, close quotation). Click on **&** and double-click on **CustomerZip**. Remove the **<<Expr>>** that was automatically inserted just after the **CustomerCompAddress** field name from the expression. (Note that you may have more than one appearance of **<<Expr>>**. You will need to remove every instance for your expression to run properly.)

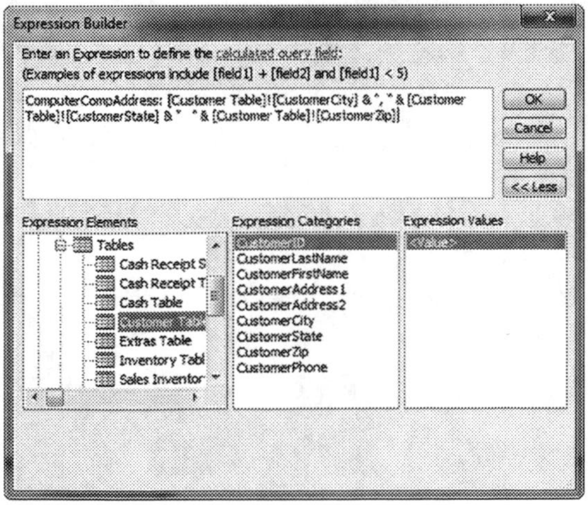

FIGURE 4-22

28. Click **OK** and click the **Run** ![Run] icon in the **Results** section of the **Design** tab (Figure 4-23).

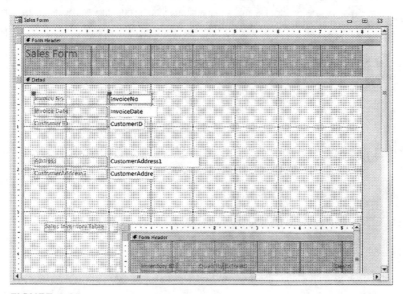

Invoice No	Invoice Date	Customer ID	Last Name	First Name	Address	CustomerAc	City	State	Zip Code	ComputerCc	Custom
2	9/5/2012	BR113	Brodie	John	7312 Veranda \		Sherman Oaks	CA	91423-	Sherman Oaks, John Br
3	9/7/2012	XA100	Xavier	Matthew	922 Outlaw Cor		Stockton	CA	95210-	Stockton, CA Matthe
4	9/10/2012	VO211	Votaw	Ryan	635 Stone Cour		San Diego	CA	92123-	San Diego, CA Ryan V
5	9/11/2012	SA114	Sawyer	Margaret	22 Silversmith		Santa Cruz	CA	95062-	Santa Cruz, CA Margar
6	9/13/2012	KL156	Klein	Jimmy	65 Sinclair Driv		Seaside	CA	93955-	Seaside, CA 9 Jimmy
7	9/14/2012	RE101	Reynolds	Quentin	1900 Greenlaw: Apt. 3A		Cary	NC	27519-	Cary, NC 2751 Quenti
8	9/18/2012	GA435	Garcia	Jorges	453 Main Stree		Potter Valley	CA	95469-	Potter Valley, Jorges
9	9/18/2012	HE100	Hess	Kelly	553 West Reefs		Oceanside	CA	92055-	Oceanside, CA Kelly H
10	9/18/2012	SA114	Sawyer	Margaret	22 Silversmith		Santa Cruz	CA	95062-	Santa Cruz, CA Margar
11	9/20/2012	CA003	Cameron	Casey	12773 Calma Cr		La Selva Beach	CA	96076-	La Selva Beach, Casey (
12	9/21/2012	CH076	Chen	Max	876 River Road		Escondido	CA	92027-	Escondido, CA Max Ch
13	9/21/2012	JO100	Jones	Rachel	439 Calma Lane		San Diego	CA	92128-	San Diego, CA Rachel
14	9/24/2012	TR186	Tran	Hui	7468 W. Yorkshi Apt. 501		La Mesa	CA	91943-	La Mesa, CA 9 Hui Tra
15	9/24/2012	CA121	Calnan	Andrea	1210 Londonde		Potters Bar	CA	92126-	Potters Bar, CA Andrea
16	9/25/2012	KL156	Klein	Jimmy	65 Sinclair Driv		Seaside	CA	93955-	Seaside, CA 3 Jimmy
17	9/25/2012	TA152	Tanaka	George	130 Parkway Bl		Riverside	CA	92518-	Riverside, CA George
18	9/25/2012	KU065	Kurosawa	Hideaki	5 Columbus Lar		Fremont	CA	94539-	Fremont, CA Hideak
19	9/26/2012	CA003	Cameron	Casey	12773 Calma Cr		La Selva Beach	CA	96076-	La Selva Beach, Casey C

FIGURE 4-23

29. Return to the **Design View** for the **Query Builder**. Make another composite field for the customer's name using the same process you followed in Step 23. Put the **FirstName** field first and the **LastName** field second with a space in between (" "). Name this field **CustomerCompName**.

30. Close the Query Builder (by clicking the **X** in the upper right hand corner) and save the query.

31. Highlight on the **LastName** label and field; right-click on them and click Delete. Repeat the process and delete the **FirstName**, **CustomerCity**, **CustomerState**, and **CustomerZip** fields and their labels (Figure 4-24).

FIGURE 4-24

32. Click on the **Add Existing Fields** icon in the **Tools** section of the **Design** tab. A **Field List** window appears with all the fields that are available for this form (Figure 4-25). Notice that the two new fields that you created are in this list.

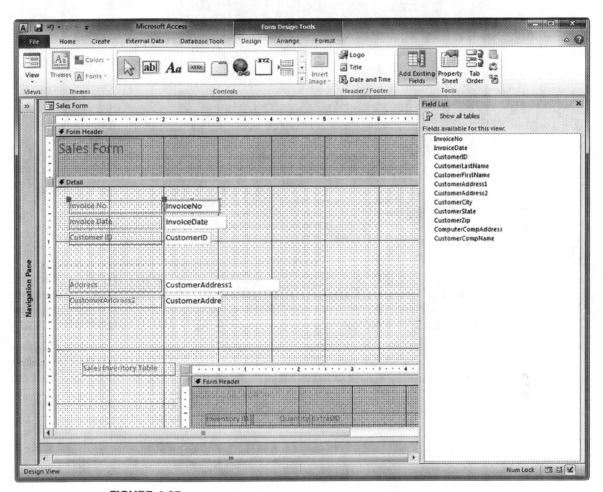

FIGURE 4-25

33. Click on the **CustomerCompName** field and drag it to the right of the **InvoiceNo** field. Drag the **CustomerAddress1** field below the **CustomerCompName** field and drop it and then drag the **CustomerAddress2** field below the **CustomerAddress1** field. Now drag the new **CustomerCompAddress** field from the **Field List** below the **CustomerAddress2** field.

34. Delete the labels on the customer name and address fields by clicking on them and hitting the delete key (or right click on the label and select **Cut**). Be careful not to delete the fields themselves. Adjust the size of the new fields (Figure 4-26).

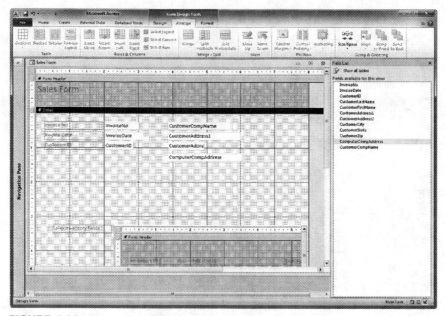

FIGURE 4-26

You can close the **Field List** now. Since the **Customer Table** is one of the tables that data is read from in this form, we need to ensure that the user cannot write any data to the **Customer Table** in this particular application. Therefore, we now want to format the customer fields so that the user cannot change the data that is entered in these fields.

35. Place the cursor below the lower right-hand corner of the **CustomerComp-Address** field. Hold down the left mouse button and drag the cursor across all of the customer fields until you have drawn a rectangle across all of the fields. When you release the cursor, all of the customer fields should be highlighted (Figure 4-27).

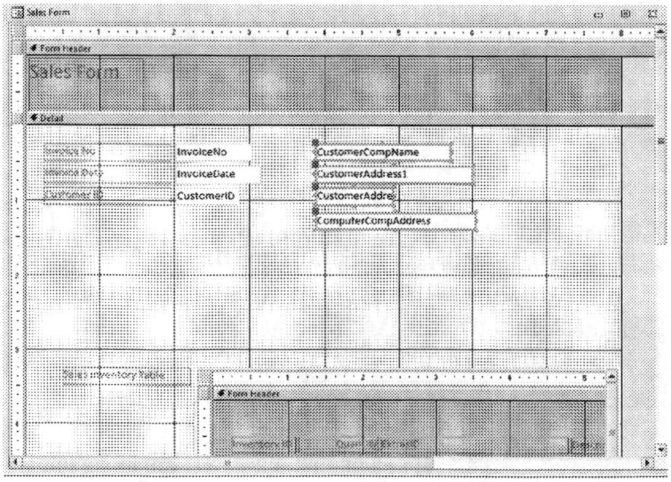

FIGURE 4-27

36. We want the Customer information to automatically appear when the **Customer ID** is entered. This is called *closed-loop verification*, where one item of data is used to retrieve other fields from a record so the user can ensure that the proper record has been accessed. While it is not necessarily a very strong internal control, it is a good preventive control to ensure that the wrong customer does not get billed. To achieve closed-loop verification, click on the **Property Sheet** icon in the **Tools** section of the **Design** tab.

The **Property Sheet** window is now accessible on the right-hand side of the screen. If it does not open to the **Data** tab, click on the **Data** tab now. Change the **Enabled** property to **No**. This results in deactivating the property and it will appear dimmer than the other properties. We don't want the values in these fields to be dimmer than the other fields, though. Therefore, we will also change the **Locked** property to **Yes**. When the **Locked** property is set to **Yes**, the field value can't be edited. Using a combination of these two properties results in leaving the data readable but prevents users from making changes to the values contained in them (Figure 4-28).

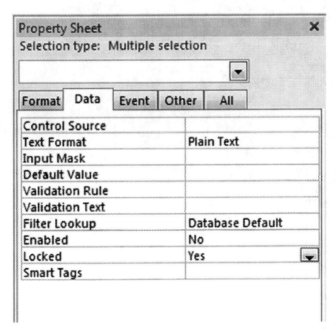

FIGURE 4-28

37. Click on the **Other** tab and click on **Tab Stop** and change it to **No**. This will reduce confusion for the user by ensuring that the cursor does not stop on the disabled fields.

38. Click on the **Format** tab and click on **Back Color**. Click on the Build button and choose a color that will blend with the style of the form you choose. (For example, if your Form back color is white, you might want to choose white for the **Back Color**.) Click on **Border Style** and select **Transparent** from the pull-down menu (Figure 4-29). Close the **Property Sheet** window.

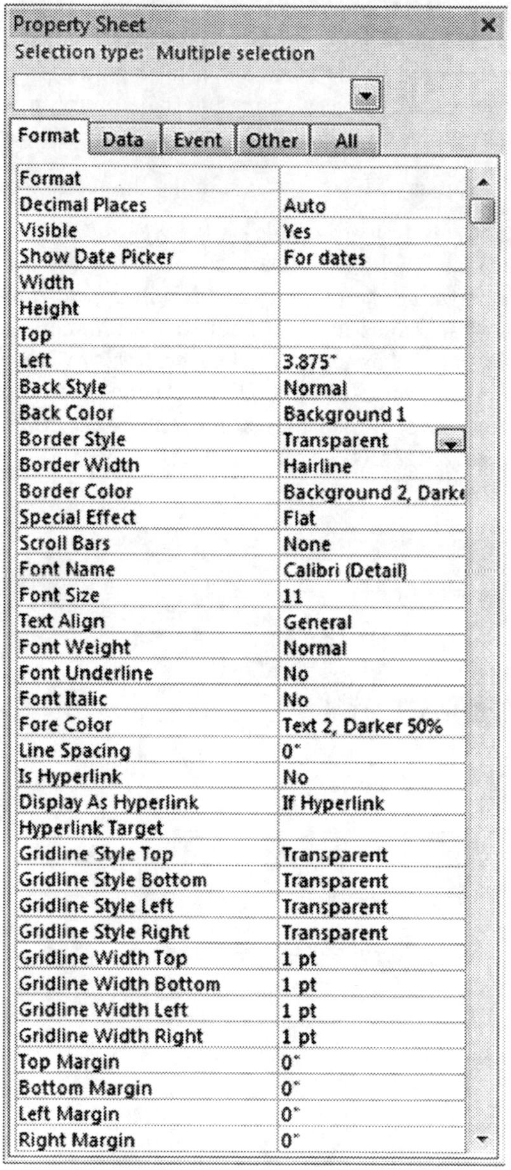

Property Sheet ✕
Selection type: Multiple selection

Format	Data	Event	Other	All

Format	
Decimal Places	Auto
Visible	Yes
Show Date Picker	For dates
Width	
Height	
Top	
Left	3.875"
Back Style	Normal
Back Color	Background 1
Border Style	Transparent
Border Width	Hairline
Border Color	Background 2, Darke
Special Effect	Flat
Scroll Bars	None
Font Name	Calibri (Detail)
Font Size	11
Text Align	General
Font Weight	Normal
Font Underline	No
Font Italic	No
Fore Color	Text 2, Darker 50%
Line Spacing	0"
Is Hyperlink	No
Display As Hyperlink	If Hyperlink
Hyperlink Target	
Gridline Style Top	Transparent
Gridline Style Bottom	Transparent
Gridline Style Left	Transparent
Gridline Style Right	Transparent
Gridline Width Top	1 pt
Gridline Width Bottom	1 pt
Gridline Width Left	1 pt
Gridline Width Right	1 pt
Top Margin	0"
Bottom Margin	0"
Left Margin	0"
Right Margin	0"

FIGURE 4-29

Now that we have taken care of the main portion of the **Sales Form**, we need to work on modifying the subform.

39. First, we want to delete the subform label. Again, right click on the label and then click on **Delete**. Click on the subform so that the crosshairs appear. Drag the subform up and to the left side of the main form (Figure 4-30).

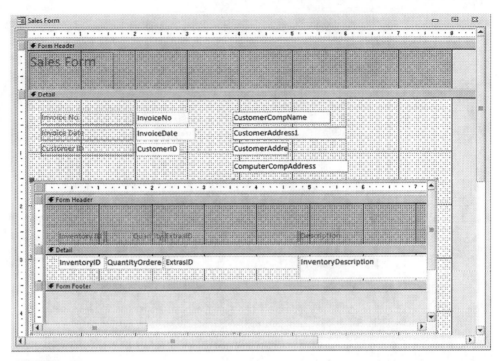

FIGURE 4-30

40. Notice that the order of the fields appears to be somewhat chaotic. We will need to adjust this. You will not need the **ExtrasID** field. You can highlight the field and label and delete them. Move the remaining fields to the right.

41. Examine the labels for **Quantity** and **InventoryPrice**. Notice that they are right justified. Click inside the **Quantity** label and click on the **Align Left** ≣ in the **Text Formatting** section of the **Home** tab to left justify this label. Do the same thing for the **InventoryPrice** label.

42. The **QuantityOrdered** text field and label and the **InventoryPrice** text field and label are larger than they will need to be. Adjust their size to make them smaller by clicking on each and dragging the right side of the box to the left.

43. Move the **Description** and **Price** fields to the left. Make the **Description** field smaller.

44. View the form now (Figure 4-31). It would appear that many of the other field sizes are larger than they need to be. Scroll to right of the subform first and move all the fields to the left. Then grab the design grid with your cursor and move that so that it is just to the left of the last field. Finally, move the outer edge of the subform window so that it is just outside the end of the subform design grid. Now you can shrink the main **Sales Form** design grid also.

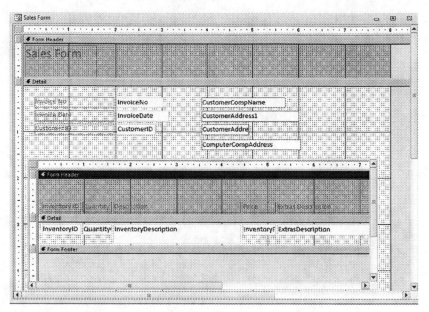

FIGURE 4-31

When the user is entering or viewing data in this form now, he or she will not have to scroll back and forth to see all the fields. They will have access to all of these fields without any additional screen movement. This facilitates completeness of data, another important internal control.

45. Just as we did not want the users to change the customer's information in the main portion of the **Sales Form**, we do not want them to change the **InventoryDescription** or the **InventoryPrice** in the subform. Right-click on the controls and select **Properties** to pull up the **Property Sheet** window. Change the properties on these two fields so that the user cannot enter or change anything.

46. Save your form at this time.

The Sales Form: Creating a Combo Box

Since there are a limited number of extra items that can be added to customize a surfboard, we can modify the subform by adding a pull-down menu called a Combo Box from which to select these extra items.

1. We will replace the **ExtrasDescription** and **ExtrasPrice** fields with a Combo Box. Delete these two fields but do not delete the label for **ExtrasDescription**. Drag the label next to the **Inventory Price** label.

2. Click on the **Combo Box** icon in the **Controls** section of the **Design** tab. Drag a rectangle in the empty area in the Detail section below the Extras Description label. The **Combo Box Wizard** window pops up (Figure 4-32). Click **Next**.

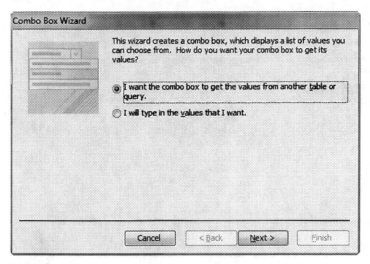

FIGURE 4-32

3. The Wizard will ask which table should provide the values for your Combo Box. Click on the **ExtrasTable** and click **Next**.

4. In the next window, select the **ExtrasID**, **ExtrasDescription** and **ExtrasPrice** fields (Figure 4-33). Click **Next**.

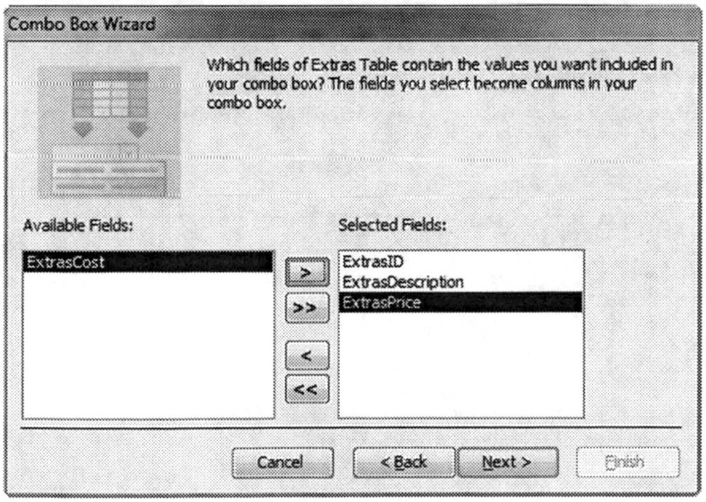

FIGURE 4-33

5. The following window (Figure 4-34) allows us to choose the order in which we want the data to be displayed in the **Combo Box**. Select **ExtrasDescription** and **Ascending**. This will result in an alphabetical display of the description in the **Combo Box**. Click **Next**.

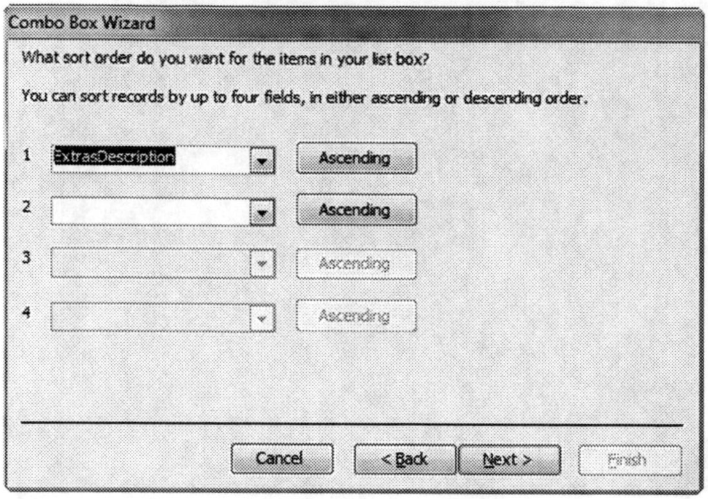

FIGURE 4-34

6. Follow the directions in the next window (Figure 4-35) to adjust the column width by double-clicking on the **Extras Description** column and the **Extras Price** column and then click **Next**. Stretch the Description field out so that you can read all the fields.

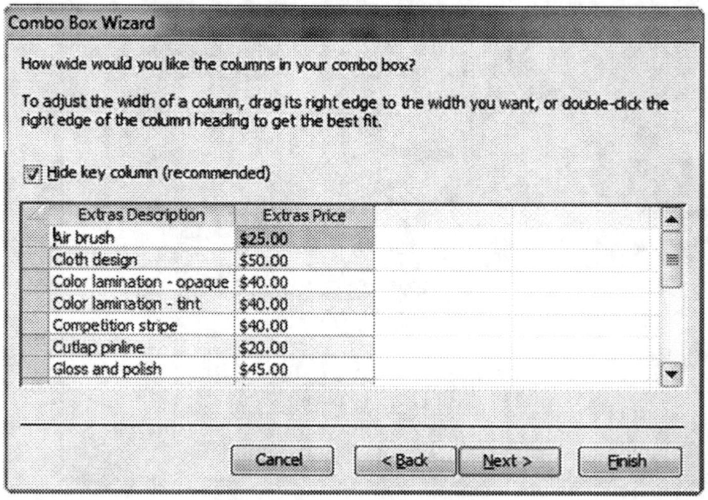

FIGURE 4-35

7. We can either have the values remembered for later use or stored in a field. Click on **Store that value in this field** and select **ExtrasID** from the pull-down menu (Figure 4-36). This binds the data that is selected in the Sales Form to the Extras Table. Click on **Next**.

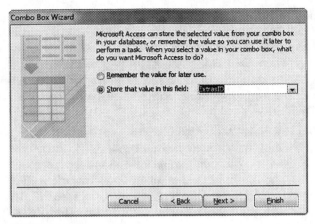

FIGURE 4-36

8. Finally, the label for the Combo Box should be **Extras Description**. Click **Finish**.

9. We already have a label for the newly created Combo Box so we can delete the new one. Be careful not to delete the Combo Box.

10. Open the form in **Form View** and examine your new **Combo Box** by clicking on the pull-down menu to ensure that all descriptions are clearly visible (Figure 4-37). The **Column Widths** can be adjusted by returning to the **Design View**, right-clicking on the **Combo Box** and selecting **Properties**. This will pull up the Property Sheet for **Combo Box**. The Column Widths property can be found under the **Format** tab. The 0" refers to the left margin. The next figure refers to the width of the first column, etc. Changing these amounts will adjust the width of the columns individually. Alternatively, you can drag out the length of the entire Combo Box, which will increase the width of all columns proportionately.

Property Sheet	✕
Selection type: Combo Box	
Combo14	▾

Format	Data	Event	Other	All

Format	
Decimal Places	Auto
Visible	Yes
Column Count	3
Column Widths	0";1.8438";0.5"
Column Heads	No
List Rows	16
List Width	2.3438"
Separator Characters	System Separator
Width	2.5417"
Height	0.2188"
Top	0.0417"
Left	5.2083"
Back Style	Normal
Back Color	Background 1
Border Style	Solid
Border Width	Hairline

FIGURE 4-37

11. We need to extend the price of the ordered surfboard. To do this, we will have to create a new field. Right-click on the subform's selector box (between the two rulers). Select **Form Properties** from the pull-down menu to obtain the **Property Sheet** for the subform. Click on **Data** tab. Click on the **Build** [...] button next to **Record Source**. As you are aware, there are three tables in the subform: the **Sales Inventory Table**, the **Inventory Table**, and the **Extras Table**. These three tables are present in the upper portion of the **Query Builder**.

12. Scroll to the left of the design grid until you reach an open column. Click in the Field cell of this column and click on the **Builder** ⚒ Builder icon. Type **Extension:** in the upper part of the window. Click on the Database in the far left window to open it. (See Figure 4-38.) Then click on Tables and select the **Sales Inventory Table**. Double-click on **QuantityOrdered** in the middle window. Click on * and type "(" (typed as open parentheses). Select the **Inventory Table**. Double-click on **InventoryPrice**. Type " + " (typed as plus sign). Select the **Extras Table** in the far left lower window. Double-click on **ExtrasPrice**. Type ")" (typed as close parentheses). Remove the **<< Expr >>** that was automatically inserted just after the **Extension** field name from the expression. Click **OK**.

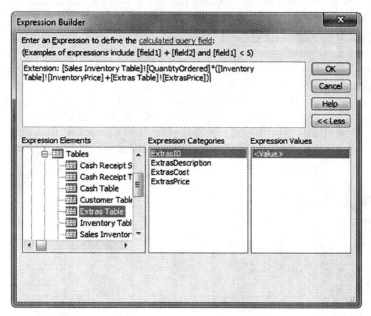

FIGURE 4-38

13. Click on **Run** ! and close and save the changes made by clicking on the **X** in the upper right-hand corner of the **Query Builder** window. Close the **Property Sheet** window.

14. Click on the **Add Existing Fields** icon in the **Tools** section of the **Design** tab. Drag the newly created **Extension** field next to the **ExtrasID** Combo Box field. Click on the Label for the Extension field. Hit **Ctrl X**. Click on the Form Header portion of the subform and hit **Ctrl V**. The **Extension** field Label is now in the upper left hand corner of the Form Header section. Drag it above the **Extension** field. Notice that the **Extension** Label has a colon after it (i.e, it reads "Extension:"). Click on the label again and delete the colon from the label. *Remember that you are creating this form for a business and that appearance and user-friendliness are important!!*

If necessary, adjust the font so that it matches the font for the other labels. In addition, you may need to adjust the width or depth of the field. Close the **Field List** window.

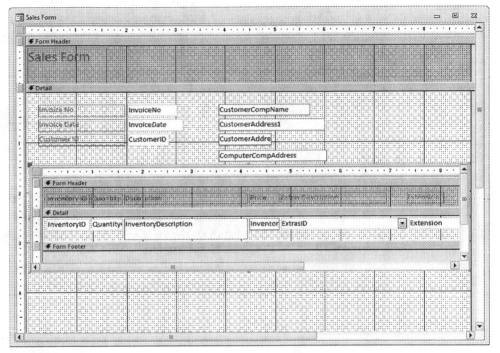

FIGURE 4-39

On occasion, a customer will order more than one surfboard. Therefore, we need to be able to arrive at a total on the **Sales Form**.

15. If necessary, stretch the **Sales Form** downward to make room to stretch the subform downward. You can do this by dragging the upper edge of the **Form Footer** downward to extend the Detail section of the **Sales Form**. (See Figure 4-39.)

16. Highlight the entire subform and extend it downward to make room for a field in the Form Footer section. Pull down the Form Footer section by placing the cursor below the Form Footer bar until the crosshairs appear and drag the cursor down approximately ½ inch.

17. Click on the **Text Box** ![ab] icon in the **Control**s section of the **Design** tab and drag a rectangle in the **Form Footer** section so that it is placed under the **Extension** field (Figure 4-40).

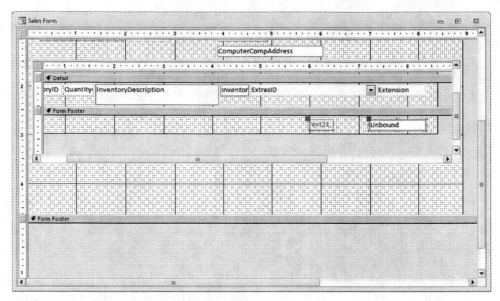

FIGURE 4-40

18. Click in the newly created Text Box and type =**Sum([Extension])**.

19. Right click on the Text Box and click on **Properties** to open the **Property Sheet**. Click on the **Format** tab and click on the **Format** property. Pull down the menu and select **Currency**. Close the **Property Sheet** window.

20. Click on the label for the newly created Text Box. Change the label to **Total**. (See Figure 4-41.) This will sum all of the extended amounts in the Detail section of the subform.

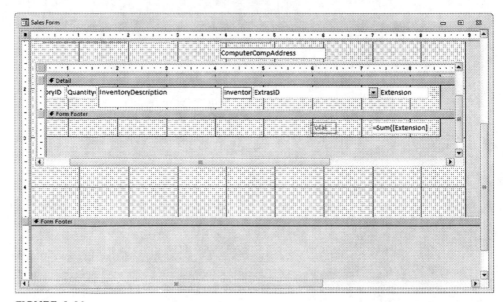

FIGURE 4-41

21. Close and save the form and subform.

22. Reopen the sales form. Use the navigation buttons at the bottom of the Sales Form to go to a **New (blank) record** ▶, i.e., a new Sales Form. Be sure you have done this for the Sales Form and not the subform.

23. Create a sale for Kevin Killian dated October 1, 2012. He is an existing customer. His **CustomerID** is KI110. He wishes to purchase a 10'6" Nice Devil surfboard. He has provided a paint sample for a custom paint job. After a search of the inventory, you discover that there is a clear 10'6" x 23 5/8" x 3 3/8" Nice Devil in stock. The **InventoryID** is ND0488. He also wishes to add a cloth design to the surfboard.

The Sales Invoice: Creating a Simple Report Based on a Query

The Sales Form we created is very useful for internal purposes; that is, it facilitates data entry. However, most customers also want to have a copy of their Sales Invoice. This requires a more formal document and, therefore, more formatting than we can provide with the **Sales Form**. We use the **Report** object in *Access* to create the **Sales Invoice Report**. First, however, we need to gather the information necessary for the **Sales Invoice Report**. We do this by building a **Sales Invoice Query**.

1. Access provides two vehicles for the creation of a query: using the Query Wizard, which is very similar to using the Form Wizard, or using Query Design, which is very similar to using Form Design as we did in Chapter 3. Click on the Query Design icon in the Queries section of the Create tab (Figure 4-42).

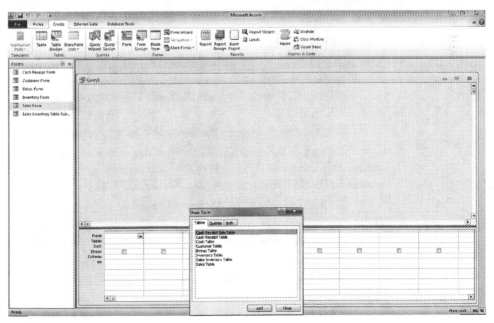

FIGURE 4-42

2. Notice that there are no tables showing in the upper half of the window. Unlike the queries that we have seen before that have been based upon pre-existing relationships, *Access* must now be told what tables to include in this query.

3. Highlight the **Sales Table**, the **Customer Table**, the **Sales Inventory Table**, the **Inventory Table**, and the **Extras Table** in the **Show Table** window and click **Add**. (See Figure 4-43.) Click **Close**.

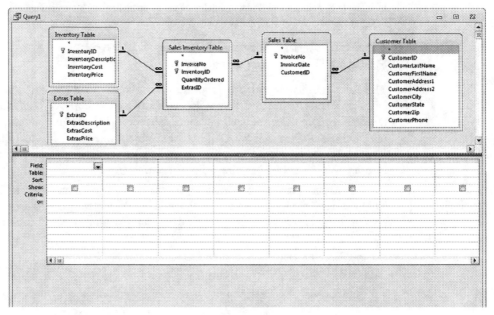

FIGURE 4-43

4. Drag all three fields from the **Sales Table** into the first three fields in the design grid.

5. Set the **Sort** property for **InvoiceNo** to Ascending.

6. Drag **CustomerLastName**, **CustomerFirstName**, **CustomerAddress1**, **CustomerAddress2**, **CustomerCity**, **CustomerState**, and **Customer Zip** from **Customer Table** into the next fields. (See Figure 4-44.)

7. Drag **InventoryID**, **QuantityOrdered**, and **ExtrasID** from **Sales Inventory Table** into the next fields.

8. Drag **InventoryDescription** and **InventoryPrice** from **Inventory Table** into the next two fields.

9. Drag **ExtrasDescription** and **ExtrasPrice** from **Extras Table** into the next two fields.

10. As we did in the **Sales Form**, we need to create a **CustomerCompAddress** and **CustomerCompName**.

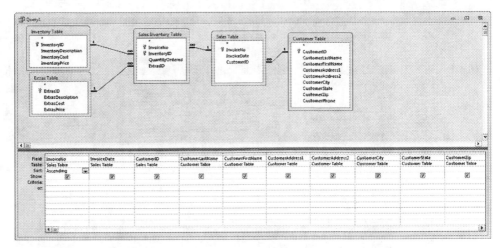

FIGURE 4-44

11. Click on the **Run** 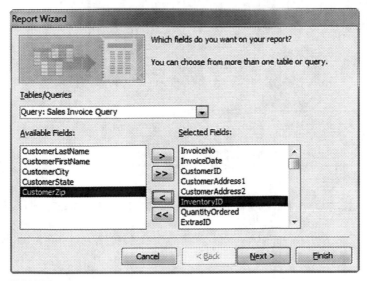 icon. Close the Query Builder and save your changes as **Sales Invoice Query**.

Now that we have gathered the information together, we are ready to create the **Sales Invoice Report**.

12. Click on the **Report Wizard** icon in the **Reports** section of the **Create** tab.

13. Select **Query: Sales Invoice Query**.

14. Click on **>>** to select all the fields. (See Figure 4-45.) Return **CustomerLastName**, **CustomerFirstName**, **CustomerCity**, **CustomerState**, and **CustomerZip** to the **Available Fields** window.

FIGURE 4-45

15. Click **Next** (Figure 4-46). We will accept the data grouped as the Report Wizard has done.

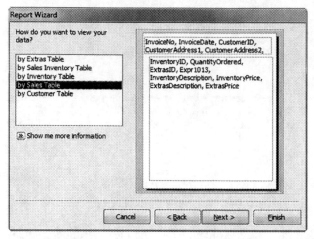

FIGURE 4-46

16. Click **Next**. We do not need to add any additional grouping levels. Therefore, we will click **Next** in the next window.

17. Choose **InventoryID** from the pull-down menu to sort the inventory in ascending order (Figure 4-47). Click on **Next**.

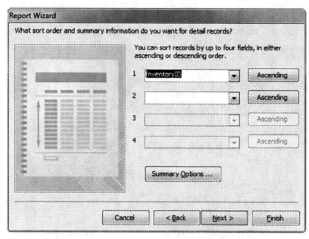

FIGURE 4-47

18. We need to choose the layout for the **Sales Invoice Report** in the next window. Click on each of the radial buttons to see how the layout of the invoice changes. Choose one of the layouts and click **Next**. Note that we have chosen Block and left the Orientation as Portrait for our report. (See Figure 4-48.)

19. Change the report name to **Sales Invoice Report** and click on **Modify the report's design**. Click **Finish**.

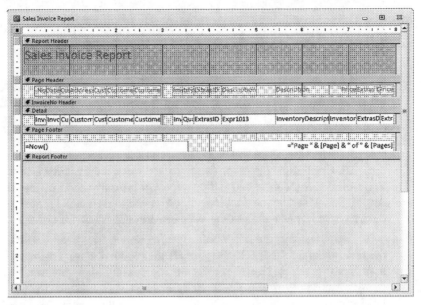

FIGURE 4-48

20. Before deciding what modifications are necessary to the **Sales Invoice Report**, we need to examine it. Click on the **View** icon and click on **Report View**.

21. We can see that we have several invoices printed on one page and many of the fields are truncated (i.e., they have been cut short). (See Figure 4-49.)

FIGURE 4-49

Click on the **View** ⬚ icon again and select **Design View** to modify the report. As we proceed through the modification of the report, we will examine the various sections of the report and discuss their purpose.

22. Just as when we created a Form, *Access* superimposed a layout on the Report when we created it. Therefore, if we want to move any of the labels or fields individually, we will first need to remove the control over the layout. Highlight all the fields and labels by dragging your cursor over them at this time. Click on the **Remove** icon in the **Control Layout** section of the **Arrange** tab.

23. Click on the top of the **Detail** section bar and drag it downward about 1 1/4 inches. The **Detail** section is the body of the report. It typically will only appear once in a report. As you undoubtedly noticed, however, when you looked at the report in **Report View**, our report had the details of all of the sales invoices under one **Sales Invoice Report** heading.

24. Notice that the title, "Sales Invoice Report," is in the **Report Header** section of the report (Figure 4-50). The **Report Header** section is used to place information on the first page of a report. However, we could be printing many invoices and we want the title to appear at the beginning of every Sales Invoice. Therefore, we will need to move the label control from the **Report Header** section to the **InvoiceNo Header** (defined later) section. If we were creating a report for Financial Statements, the information for the title page would go in the **Report Header** section.

25. Drag the bottom of the **InvoiceNo Header** bar down to make room for the title that we want to place in this section. Highlight the label in the Report Header section by double-clicking on the outer edge of the rectangle or by dragging your cursor across the entire rectangle. Drag it to the top of the **InvoiceNo Header** section. The **InvoiceNo Header** provides header information based upon every new invoice number. Therefore, having a Sales Invoice title appear would be appropriate. However, we don't need the word "Report" in the title; modify the label to eliminate the word "Report."

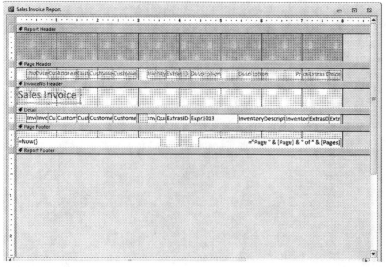

FIGURE 4-50

26. As we discussed, we don't need the **Report Header** or **Report Footer** sections for Sales Invoices so we can remove them now. Right click on the **Report Header** or **Report Footer** section bar and select **Report Header/Footer** to remove them from the report.

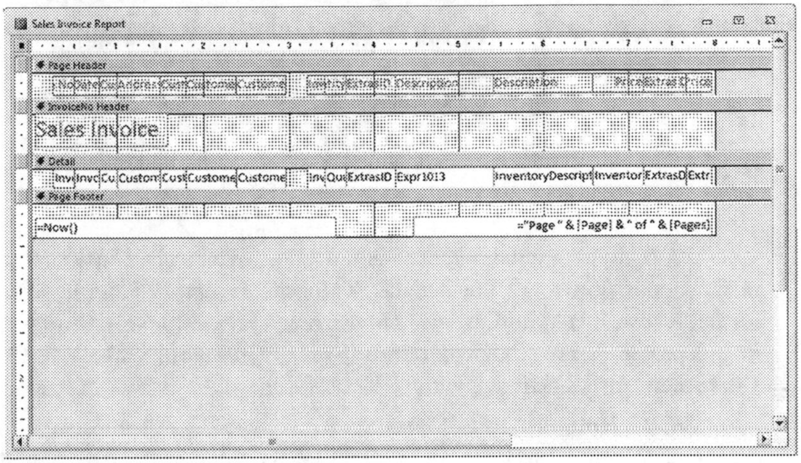

FIGURE 4-51

27. The field labels are in the **Page Header** section (Figure 4-51). The **Page Header** section is an area in which we can add page numbers or column headings in a report. However, we want the labels to be associated with each Sales Invoice so we will move them to the **InvoiceNo Header** section. Place your cursor to the right of all the labels in the **Page Header** section and drag it to the left so that you select all of the labels in that section. Drag them into the **InvoiceNo Header** section so that they are aligned directly above the fields in the **Detail** section bar (Figure 4-52).

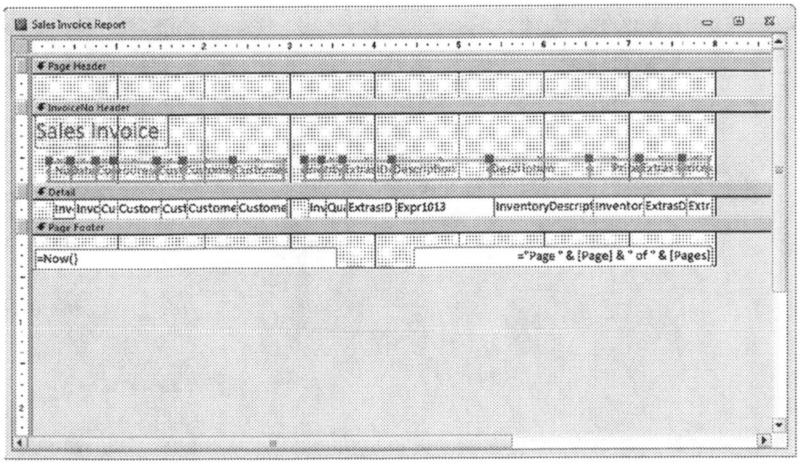

FIGURE 4-52

28. We don't need the **Page Header** section so we can delete that now. Right click on the **Page Header** or **Page Footer** section bar and click on **Page Header/Footer**. Click the **Yes** button to confirm the deletion (Figure 4-53).

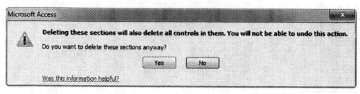

FIGURE 4-53

29. Now we are ready to format the Sales Invoice. The customer information belongs in the upper portion of the invoice, while the inventory information belongs in tabular format below. In addition, we need to rearrange the customer information so that it appears in the proper order (**CustomerCompName**, **CustomerAddress1**, **CustomerAddress2**, **CustomerCompAddress**), with all fields on the right side of the invoice.

30. Extend the **Detail** section bar down 1 ½ inches to make room for the customer information. Drag all the field labels down to the top of the **Detail** section bar. Drag the **CustomerCompName**, **CustomerAddress1**, **CustomerAddress2**, and **CustomerCompAddress** fields into the **InvoiceNo Header** section, arranging them neatly in order on right side of the section (Figure 4-54). Delete their labels.

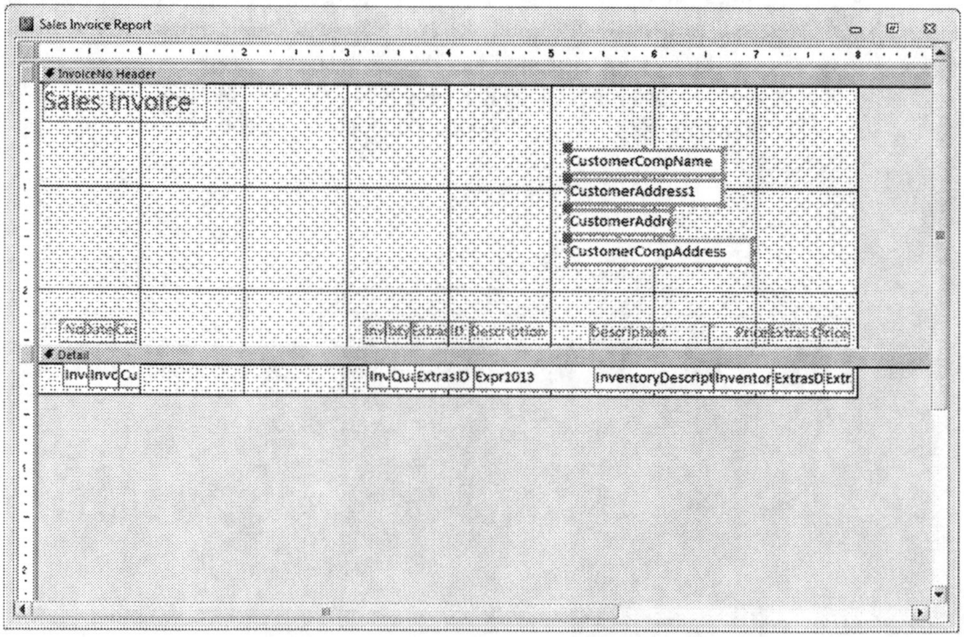

FIGURE 4-54

31. Drag the **InvoiceNo**, **InvoiceDate**, and **CustomerID** fields and their labels to the left side of the **InvoiceNo Header** section and arrange these fields neatly (Figure 4-55). Move the remaining fields to the left and adjust their length. Note that, just as we didn't need the **ExtrasID** field in the **Sales Form**, we also don't need it here. You can delete this field.

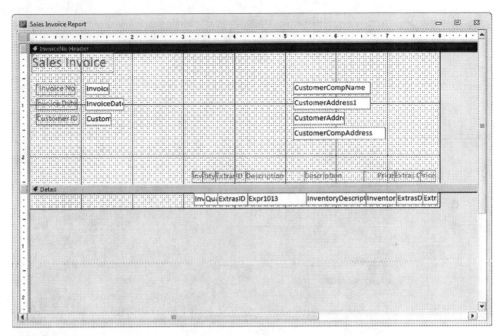

FIGURE 4-55

32. We know we have to fit all the fields in a sheet of paper that is 8 ½" wide and that, if the **Sales Invoice** is going to look professional, we need to leave space for a margin of ¾" to 1" on each side of the page. Using your ruler at the top of the page as a guide, place the customer information so that it will fall within 6 inches of the grid. This is critical! If your fields fall outside of this, extra pages will be printed when Tragg's prints their invoices! For example, let's assume you allow the **CustomerCompAddress** field to stretch beyond the 6.5" mark. Even if there were no characters filling that blank area in the space that you allowed for the field, *Access* would print an extra page for the overflow. If there were characters in that space, those extra characters would appear by themselves on the additional page. You can see why spacing is extremely important in designing these reports.

33. We can now move the remaining fields and labels to the left and provide some space between them. As we do this, it is important to keep referring to how the invoices look in Report View. Make sure that none of the fields are truncated (i.e., none of the data is cut off). Make sure that the spacing between the fields is equal. Keep all the fields within the 6.5 inches discussed in the step above.

34. In looking at Figure 4-56 in **Report View**, we can see that the **Description** field is truncated. We can extend the length of the field or we can extend the depth of the field.

Since we also need to create a field that will total the price of the surfboard and its extras and the width of the report is an issue, we will increase the depth of the description fields rather than increasing the length of these fields. Drag the bottom of the **Detail** section down about ¼".

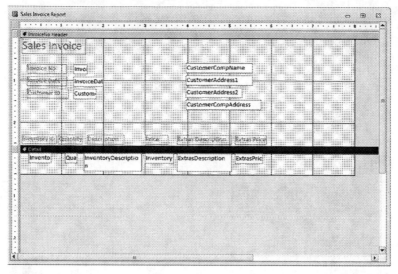

FIGURE 4-56

35. Now we are ready to extend the price of each surfboard purchased. Click on the **Text Box** [ab] icon and draw a rectangle in the space you have made at the right of the Detail section. Right click inside the **Text Box** and click on **Properties** to pull up the **Property Sheet** window (Figure 4-57). Click on the **Data** tab. In the **Control Source** property, type: = **[QuantityOrdered]*([InventoryPrice] + [ExtrasPrice])**.

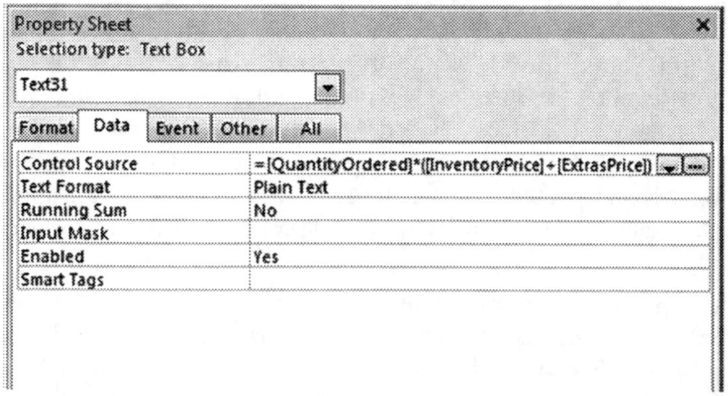

FIGURE 4-57

36. Click on the **Other** tab. Change the **Name** property to **ReportExtension**. Click on the **Format** tab. Change the **Format** property to **Currency**. Close the **Property Sheet** window.

37. Right click on the label that was automatically created in the detail section of the form. Click **Cut**. Now click in the InvoiceNo Header section of the form and click Paste. Change the Label to "Extension." Move the label so that it is above its field. Use the **Format Painter** ✐ icon in the **Font** section of the **Design** tab to format the Extension label so that it appears to be the same as the other field labels.

38. We still need a total for the **Sales Invoice**. Right click on the **Detail** section bar (Figure 4-58). Click on the **Sorting and Grouping** option. Note that we are already grouping on the InvoiceNo.

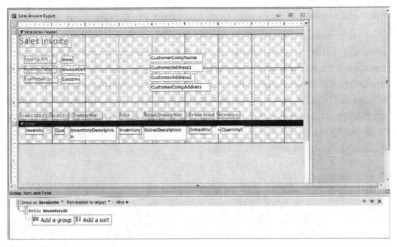

FIGURE 4-58

39. Select the **More** More ▸ icon and change the grouping options to **with a footer section** and **keep whole group together on one page**. (See Figure 4-59.) Close the **Sorting and Grouping Dialog Box**.

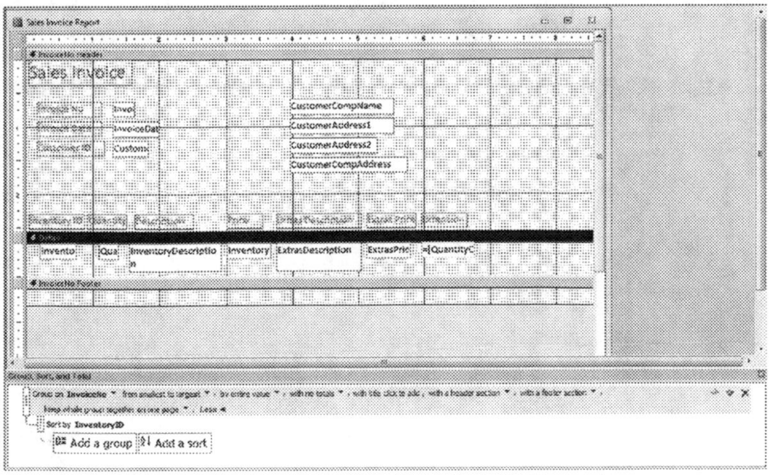

FIGURE 4-59

40. Stretch the newly created footer downward approximately ¼ inch. Create a **Text Box**. Right click on the **Text Box** and pull up the **Property Sheet** window. Type = **Sum([QuantityOrdered]*([InventoryPrice] + [ExtrasPrice]))** in the **Control Source** of this box. Change the **Name** property to **InvoiceTotal** and change the **Format** property to **Currency**.

41. Click on the Label attached to the **Text Box** and change it to **Invoice Total**. Format this label so that it stands out.

42. We need to make sure we print only one invoice per page. Right click on the **InvoiceNo Footer**, click on **Properties** and click on the **Format** tab. Change the **Force New Page** property to **After Section**. Close the **Property Sheet** window.

43. Finally, we need to center the fields in the Sales Invoice. Before you close and save the **Sales Invoice Report**, switch to the **Print Preview** to be sure that the **Sales Invoice** looks professional. (See Figure 4-60.) Adjust the margins if it needs to be centered horizontally or vertically on the pages. Be sure that only one **Sales Invoice** is printing on a page and there are no blank pages printing between invoices. This may seem to be a trivial matter. However, wasted paper can become a big expense to a company. To be sure you have no blank pages, adjust your page width to 7 ½ inches and make sure that you leave a ¾ to 1" margin on the left side.

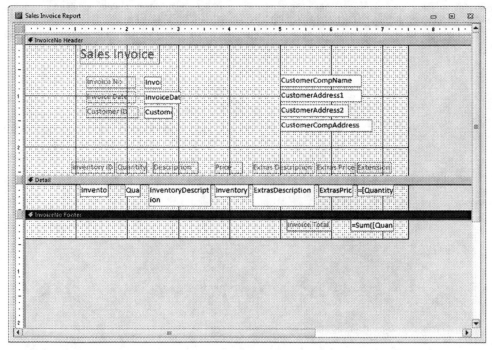

FIGURE 4-60

In the **Print Preview** view of the report, you will be able to see exactly how the report will look when it prints (Figure 4-61).

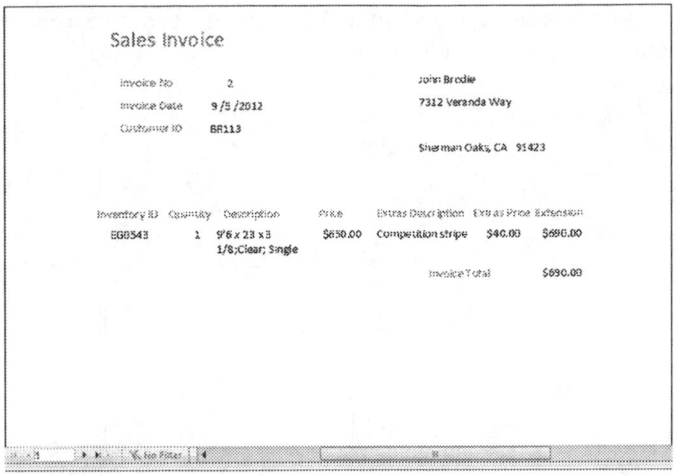

FIGURE 4-61

Queries with Simple Criteria

There are various types of queries that provide useful information in the Sales/Collection Business Process. We created some of these queries while building the **Sales Form** and **Sales Report** in the previous exercises. In addition, both internal and external users often need to query the database to obtain information. For example, Dan Tragg may wish to obtain a list of each inventory item and its selling price to determine whether they are low on any particular type of surfboard. To obtain this information, we would use a *Select Query*. A select query is the most commonly used type of query. It retrieves rows of data from one or more tables and displays the results in a dynaset. The select query can be enhanced to group records and calculate sums, averages, and other totals.

As with many queries of resources, obtaining the inventory list for Tragg's Custom Surfboard is relatively easy and requires the use of only one table.

1. Click on **Query Design** icon in the **Queries** section of the **Create** tab. Double click on **Inventory Table** in the **Show Table** window and click **Close** (Figure 4-62).

FIGURE 4-62

2. Drag **InventoryID**, **InventoryDescription**, and **InventoryPrice** into the first three columns of the design grid (Figure 4-63).

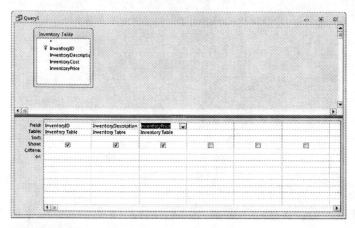

FIGURE 4-63

3. Click on the **Run** ⚡ icon. As you can tell, this is a very simple query and before we continue with it, let's take a minute to think about the "structure" of queries. We have been using a design grid and a query builder to facilitate the building of our queries thus far. However, behind the scenes, *Access* uses SQL (Structured Query Language) as the basis upon which all queries are built. If we were "fluent" in SQL, we could create all of our queries using SQL. As you should recall, the basic form for all SQL queries is:

SELECT *attributes (fields)*

FROM *Table*

WHERE *criteria are met*

If there are no criteria (as there are none in this query), there is no WHERE command. We can examine the SQL statement for any query that we make by clicking on the **View** ▦ icon and selecting **SQL View** (Figure 4-64).

FIGURE 4-64

Notice that the SELECT command contains all three fields that we dragged into the design grid and the FROM command contains the Inventory Table from which the three fields were chosen.

4. Click on the **View** icon again and chose the **Design View**. Now click on Ascending in the **Sort** property for the **InventoryID** field and click on the **Run** ⬇ icon (Figure 4-65).

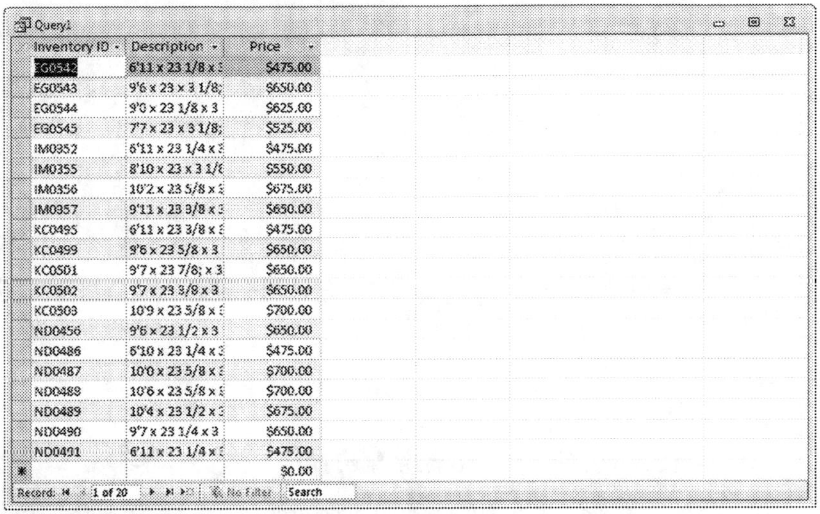

FIGURE 4-65

5. Click on the **Design View** 📐 icon again.

We can refine this query by searching for inventory on hand that are priced less than $675.00. This utilizes the Criteria property in the design grid.

6. Type < 675.00 in the Criteria property for the **InventoryPrice** field and click on the **Run** icon again (Figure 4-66).

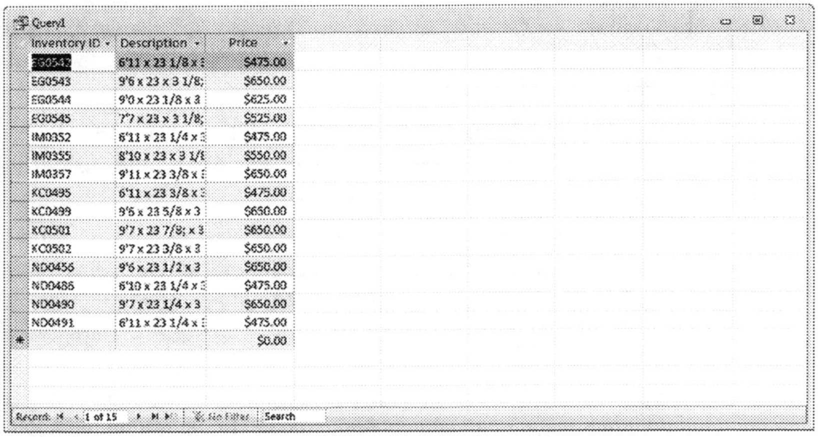

FIGURE 4-66

7. Now click on the **SQL View** once more (Figure 4-67). Since we have added the criteria of "< 675.00", the SQL statement now contains the WHERE command. It also has an advanced command, ORDER BY, for the sorting that we added.

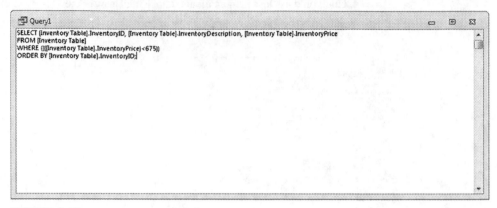

FIGURE 4-67

8. Close and save query as **Inventory Query**.

Queries with Multiple Values

A *parameter query* is one that prompts the user for the query criteria for retrieving records. These criteria can be single-valued or multi-valued. In addition, the criteria can be entered as absolute values or as wildcards. Assume that a company has a calendar year-end. We can query for all sales greater than $650.00 between January 1, 2012 and December 31, 2012. We could also create the query by using wildcards for the dates. In this case, the query would substitute variables such as "BeginDate" or "BSDate." In this parameter query, *Access* then prompts the user for the appropriate values.

Assume that Dan Tragg wants to view his Cash Receipts for October. We can easily create a query that can isolate those cash receipts but that will also be useful for querying cash receipts at any time during the year.

1. Click on the **Query Design** icon. Double click on the **Cash Receipts Table** and the **Cash Receipt Sale Table** to add them to the upper part of the **Query Design** window. Close the **Show Table** window.

2. Drag the **CashReceiptID** and **CRDate** from the **Cash Receipts Table** into the first two columns of the design grid. Drag the **AmountApplied** field from the **Cash Receipt Sale Table** into the third column of the design grid (Figure 4-68).

3. Click on the Totals Σ icon. Note the change in the design grid when you do. You now have a "Total" property in the grid. Use the pull-down menu under the Total property for the **CRDate**. Note that there are various mathematical functions (including Sum and Average) that we could choose here. However, these are not appropriate for a date field. Scroll down to the bottom of the menu. The "Where" function will allow us to set the criteria for the date. Change the Total property for the **CRDate** field to "Where", (e.g., "where" the date is between the beginning of the year and the end of the year).

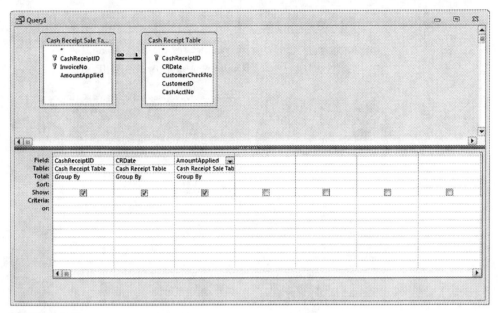

FIGURE 4-68

4. In the Criteria property of the **CRDate** field, type **Between [BeginDate] and [EndDate]**. (See Figure 4-69.)

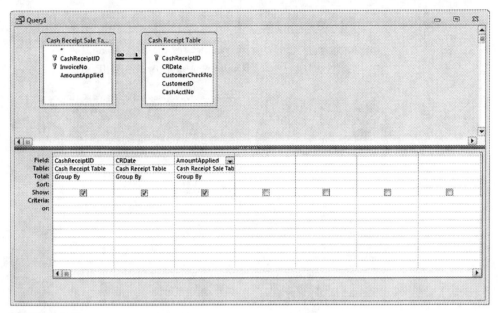

FIGURE 4-69

5. Click on the **Run** ![Run icon] icon. (See Figure 4-70.)

6. Type 1/1/2012 in the prompt for the BeginDate.

7. Type 10/31/2012 when prompted for the EndDate.

Cash Receip ▾	Amount ▾
10105	$345.00
10107	$257.00
10108	$725.00
10111	$347.50
10125	$357.50
10126	$725.00
10127	$740.00
10144	$712.50
10145	$347.50
10146	$347.50
10147	$730.00
10151	$732.50
10152	$350.00
10153	$740.00
10154	$347.50
10158	$712.50
10161	$287.50
10162	$350.00
10164	$357.50
10165	$345.00
10166	$250.00
10167	$287.50
10169	$732.50
10170	$350.00

Record: I◄ ◄ 1 of 24 ► ►I ► 🞏 No Filter | Search

FIGURE 4-70

8. Take another look at the **SQL View**. Note that since this query involves both the **Cash Receipts Table** and the **Cash Receipts Sales Table** the SQL statement now includes an INNER JOIN command (Figure 4-71).

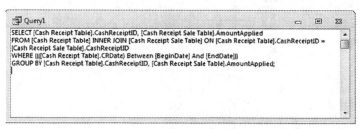

```
SELECT [Cash Receipt Table].CashReceiptID, [Cash Receipt Sale Table].AmountApplied
FROM [Cash Receipt Table] INNER JOIN [Cash Receipt Sale Table] ON [Cash Receipt Table].CashReceiptID =
[Cash Receipt Sale Table].CashReceiptID
WHERE ((([Cash Receipt Table].CRDate) Between [BeginDate] And [EndDate]))
GROUP BY [Cash Receipt Table].CashReceiptID, [Cash Receipt Sale Table].AmountApplied;
```

FIGURE 4-71

9. Save the query as **Monthly Cash Receipts Query**.

KEY TERMS

business process	design grid	Select Query
closed loop verification	Parameter Query	
combo box	Sales/Collection business process	

QUESTIONS AND PROBLEMS FOR REVIEW

4.1 To convert a conceptual model with a maximum cardinality relationship of "many to many" into relationship database tables, you must

  (a) create a foreign key in one of the tables to link the two tables.

  (b) create a relation with no attributes of its own.

  (c) create a separate table with a concatenated primary key comprised of the primary keys from both entity tables.

  (d) Many to many relationships cannot be represented in *Access*.

4.2 A control in which you can type a value or can click on a pull-down menu to display a list and then select an item from that list is called a

  (a) control box.

  (b) text box.

  (c) combo box.

  (d) source box.

  (e) None of the above.

4.3 A query that displays its own dialog box prompting the user for information for representing records is called a(n)

  (a) select query.

  (b) parameter query.

  (c) crosstab query.

  (d) action query.

  (e) None of the above.

4.4 To ensure that users cannot enter data in certain fields, the Locked and Enabled properties should be set to

  (a) locked = Yes, enabled = No.

  (b) locked = Yes, enabled = Yes.

  (c) locked = No, enabled = Yes.

  (d) locked = No, enabled = No.

PROBLEMS

*Note: Not all queries can be solved in a single step. Some of the problems below will require creating queries in multiple steps. Problems with an * are more challenging problems.*

4.1 Create a query for Tragg's Customer Surfboards to sum the cash receipts (grand dollar total for the year) as of December 31, 2012. Save the query so that you can easily provide them with this information for other months in the future.

4.2 Alter the query created in Problem 4.1 to sum the cash receipts for each customer of December 31, 2012. Save the query.

4.3 Tragg's Custom Surfboards needs to know the total number of inventory items that were sold during the month of October 2012. Create the query to provide this information. Save the query.

4.4 Tragg's also wants to know the cost of inventory sold during the month of October 2012. Create the query to provide the information. Save the query. (Hint: This query should be developed in several steps.)

4.5 Tragg's has asked you for the total sales (in dollars) for the month of October 2012. Save this query so that you can easily provide them with this information for other months in the future.

4.6 Create a query to provide a Daily Cash Summary for Tragg's Custom Surfboards showing the customer number, invoice number, date, customer check number, and amount of payment. (Note: you do not need to create a report.)

4.7 Refer to "Model the Revenue Cycle Using REA" and Footnote 8. Recreate the REA diagram (Figure 4-1) under the following changed conditions:

a. The instigation event should now be included as a key event.

b. The mutual commitment event (i.e., the custom orders) are *not* collapsed into the economic decrement event (i.e., sales).

4.8 Create a query to calculate Accounts Receivable as of December 31, 2012. Save the query.

CHAPTER 5

ACQUISITION/PAYMENT BUSINESS PROCESS

INTRODUCTION

The Acquisition/Payment business process is frequently referred to as the *expenditure transaction cycle*. The Acquisition/Payment process often includes the instigation events (i.e., purchase requisitions), the mutual commitment events (i.e., purchase orders), the economic increment events (i.e., purchase of goods or services), and the economic decrement event (i.e., the cash disbursement). We might also see an economic increment reversal event (i.e., the purchase return).

To model the Acquisition/Payment business process in a database, it will be useful to create more complex forms, reports, and queries. After completing this chapter, you should be able to use Microsoft *Access* to:

- Create an AutoNumber starting at any number you wish.
- Create an append query to add records in a dynaset to an existing table.
- Create queries involving multiple tables, derived column values, and expressions.
- Create parameter queries.
- Create forms and reports using multiple tables and queries.

ACQUISITION/PAYMENT PROCESS OVERVIEW

Basic Concepts and Definitions

We again refer to Figure 1-3 and see that the expenditure cycle interfaces with the conversion cycle, the financing cycle, and the financial reporting system. The financial reporting system interfaces with the expenditure cycle and the payroll cycle. Extending this to the framework of business processes, goods and services are acquired by a company as a result of the Acquisition/Payment process. The Acquisition/Payment process delivers those goods and services either to the Sales/Collection Process for sale and subsequent cash collection or to the Conversion Process for further processing, which in turn delivers them to the Sales/Collection Process for sale and subsequent cash collection. Once the cash is collected, it is made available to the Financing process and, in turn, is used to pay for the goods and services acquired by the Acquisition/Payment process. For this to happen, the Acquisition/Payment process must include at least one economic event that transfers goods and services into the company (i.e., an increment event) and at least one economic event that transfers out the cash (i.e., a decrement event).

The Acquisition/Payment process for all firms is similar regardless of whether the firm is engaged in manufacturing, in service, or in retail.

Tragg's Custom Surfboards

Additional Background Dan Tragg insists on using only the highest quality materials in the manufacturing of his surfboards. Tragg's uses a list of approved suppliers with whom they have established a good relationship over the years. For example, they obtain their blanks (the molds for their surfboards) from one of two vendors, SeaFoam or Clarke Foam. These companies manufacture blanks that are near perfect in density from deck to core without compromising weight. In addition, they have a wide variety of blanks. The result is that Tragg's incurs much less waste when shaping the surfboard into one of its styles.

The boards are laminated with Volan fiberglass, which is a flat-weave fiberglass cloth that resists dings. This finish also makes the boards water tight, stronger, and more durable. They outsource the application of most of the Volan fiberglass finish to a well-established glasser, Austad Glassing. Pigments and other supplies are obtained through several suppliers with whom Tragg's has been dealing over a period of years.

Model the Expenditure Cycle Using REA As we begin modeling the expenditure cycle using the REA diagram, we will focus our discussion of the expenditure cycle on the purchase of inventory (i.e., the blanks, or molds for each style of surfboard sold). Obviously, there are expenditures for goods other than inventory. For example, there are expenditures for fixed assets, for miscellaneous supplies, and for services. Similarly, there are items (i.e., fixed assets and miscellaneous supplies) that are received other than inventory. For simplicity's sake, we have chosen not to represent those in the REA diagram so that you can focus on the process of purchasing, receiving, and paying for inventory.

Since the blanks are purchased for each style of surfboard sold, Tragg's is able to use only one inventory table to record the inventory for all of its stock, both production and retail. The blanks are purchased when a production supervisor recognizes a need for inventory. The supervisor goes to his or her terminal and completes a Purchase Order Form online. This is done by selecting the vendor, the inventory item, and the amounts to be ordered. The order can be for one type of blank or for several types. The Purchase Order Form is reviewed by a Purchasing Agent. If it is approved, a Purchase Order Report is prepared, printed, and mailed to SeaFoam or Clarke Foam.

The goods are received and counted by the Receiving Clerk. The Receiving Clerk enters the date, the PO Number, and the Supplier's Invoice Number in the top portion of the form. In addition, the Clerk must enter the Inventory ID number and the quantity received in the form.

If the order is in agreement with the Purchase Order, it is scheduled for payment. A separate receiving report will be completed for each Purchase Order; however, if any goods are backordered (which happens on rare occasions), Tragg's may have to complete more than one Receiving Report for a Purchase Order. Tragg's sometimes pays for more than one invoice (receipt of inventory) with each check (cash disbursement). In addition, on occasion they have placed very large orders and have paid for those orders in installments.

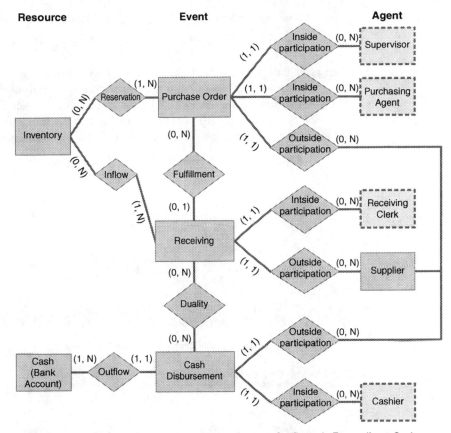

FIGURE 5-1 Basic REA Diagram for Tragg's Custom Surfboards Expenditure Cycle

Create a Relational Database for Tragg's Following the REA Diagram

Based on Figure 5-1, Tragg's table structure for the Acquisition/Payment Business Process can be represented as follows (for the sake of simplicity, we are not including those tables that are denoted by a dotted line):

Cash Table (<u>CashAcctNo</u>, AcctType)

Inventory Table (<u>InventoryID</u>, InventoryDescription, InventoryCost, InventoryPrice)

Cash Disbursement Receiving Table (<u>CashDisbursementID</u>, <u>RecRptNo</u>, AmountApplied)

PO Inventory Table (<u>PONo</u>, <u>InventoryID</u>, POQuantityOrdered)

Cash Disbursement Table (<u>CashDisbursementID</u>, CDDate, <u>SupplierID</u>, <u>CashAcctNo</u>)

Purchase Order Table (<u>PONo</u>, PODate, <u>SupplierID</u>)

Supplier Table (<u>SupplierID</u>, SupplierName, SupplierAddress1, SupplierAddress2, SupplierCity, SupplierState, SupplierZip, SupplierPhone)

Receiving Report Table (<u>RecRptNo</u>, RecRptDate, <u>PONo</u>, SupplierInvNo)

Receiving Inventory Table (<u>RecRptNo</u>, <u>InventoryID</u>, QuantityReceived)

Tragg's Relational Database using Access Open the Chapter 5 database for Tragg's Custom Surfboards from the CD. Again note that all the tables, some relationships, and some forms have already been created for the Acquisition/Payment Business Process. Before you examine the tables, forms, and the relationships that have been created thus far, please enable the content that is blocked by Access.

1. Click **Enable Content** on Security Warning bar (Figure 5-2).

FIGURE 5-2

2. Click **Yes** to make this file a Trusted Document (Figure 5-3).

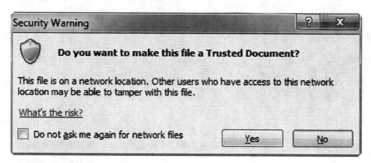

FIGURE 5-3

The Purchase Order Table and the Append Query

Recall that in Chapter 4, when we created the **Sales Form** and began entering data, the **InvoiceNo** field Data Type was set as AutoNumber. It began numbering the **Sales Forms** at 1 (which we didn't see) and continued forward from there. We do not have to begin numbering all of our forms at 1. We can number our forms at any number of our choosing. Therefore, let's assume that Tragg's would like to begin numbering the **Purchase Order Forms** at 1000.

Open the Tragg's Custom Surfboard database for Chapter 5 and take some time to acquaint yourself with the **Purchase Order Table** at this time. Notice that we have not yet set the Primary Key for this table. This is because we will be setting a default value to begin the number of the **Purchase Order Forms** and we cannot do this if the table prevents null values in the primary key field. In other words, the Required Field property cannot be set to **Yes**, and the Indexed field property cannot be set to **Yes (No Duplicates)**. Therefore, we have not yet set the Primary Key.

1. Close the **Purchase Order Table**.

2. Click on the **Table Design** icon in the **Create** section (Figure 5-4).

3. Type **PONo** in the Field Name and choose Number as the Data Type. Type 0 in the Default Value field of the Property section.

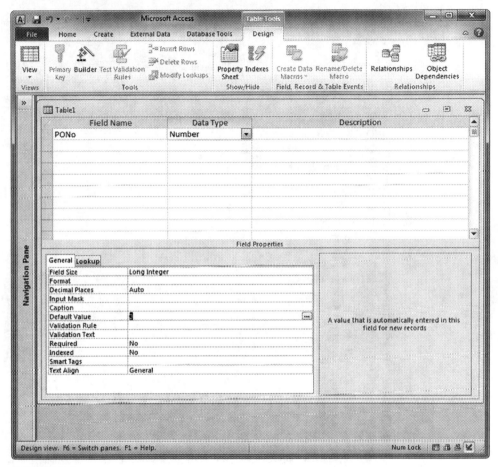

FIGURE 5-4

4. Close the table and name it **Temp PO Table**.

5. When prompted to create a primary key for this table (Figure 5-5), select **No**.

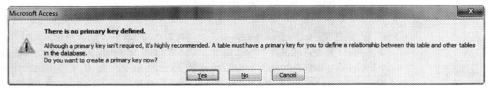

FIGURE 5-5

Open the **Temp PO Table**. In the Datasheet View, we will enter a value in the **Number** field that is one (1) less than the starting value we want for the AutoNumber field. In other words, since we want the **Purchase Order Form** to begin at 1000, we will enter 999 in this field (Figure 5-6).

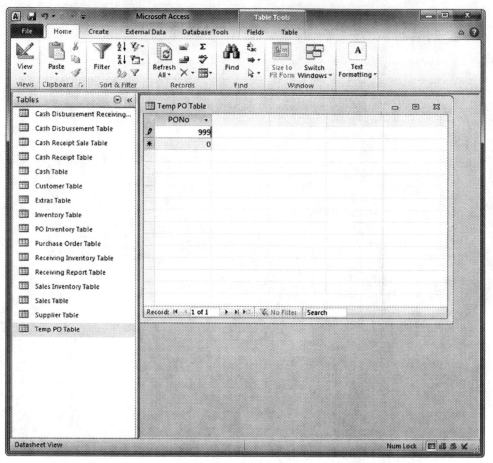

FIGURE 5-6

6. Close the table.

7. Click on the **Query Design** icon under the **Create** section.

8. Scroll down in the Show Table window and double-click **Temp PO Table**. Close the Show Table window.

9. Click on the **Append** ![Append icon] in the **Query Type** section of the **Design** tab. An Append Query adds a group of records from one or more tables to the end of one or more tables. We want *Access* to add the **PONumber** automatically each time a new Purchase Order is created. In the Table Name field, select the **Purchase Order Table**. Click **OK** (Figure 5-7).

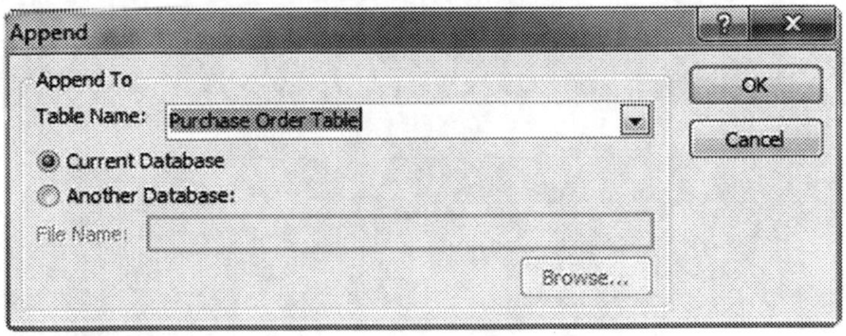

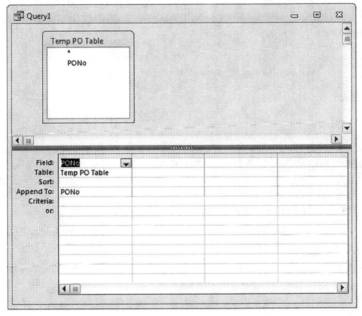

FIGURE 5-7

10. In the upper portion of the Query window, drag **PONo** from **Temp PO Table** to the first field in the design grid. Choose **PONo** in the Append To row (Figure 5-8).

FIGURE 5-8

11. Click on the **Run** ⁞_Run_ icon. A window will appear informing you that you are about to append 1 row (Figure 5-9). Click **Yes**.

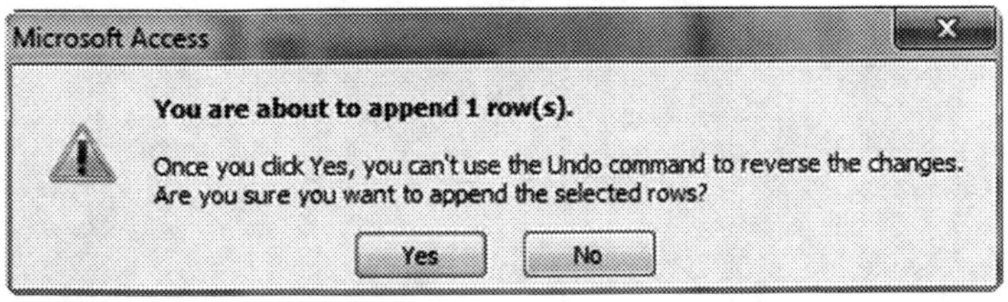

FIGURE 5-9

12. Click on the Datasheet View icon to be sure that the **Append Query** worked satisfactorily. You should see one record in the **PONo** field with 999 in it (Figure 5-10).

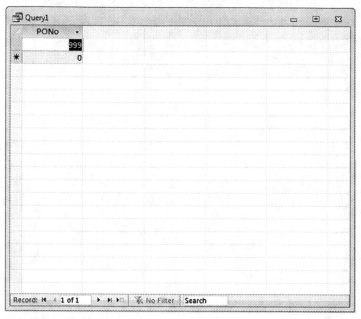

FIGURE 5-10

13. Close and save the query as **PO No Query**.

14. Click on the **Tables** object and delete the temporary table, **Temp PO Table** since we no longer need this table.

15. Open **Purchase Order Table** in **Design** view. Set **PONo** as the Primary Key. Close and save the changes to the table.

16. Double-click on the **Purchase Order Table** (Figure 5-11). You will see that 999 has now been set in the **PONo** field and the AutoNumber is ready to begin the next Purchase Order at 1000.

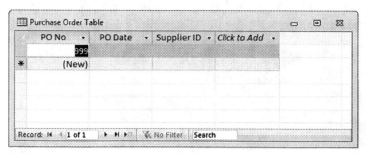

FIGURE 5-11

The Relationships: Making the Necessary Linkages

1. Examine Figure 5-1 carefully. Now that we have created the Primary Key for the **Purchase Order Table**, we need to create the necessary relationships. Click on the Relationships ⚏Relationships icon in the **Database Tools** section to open the Relationships window. Notice that we need to <u>add</u> the **Purchase Order Table** and the **PO Inventory Table**. Click on the **Show Table** 📇 icon.

2. Click on the **PO Inventory Table**, hold down the **Ctrl** key, and click on the **Purchase Order Table**. (See Figure 5-12.) Click on the **Add** key and click **Close**.

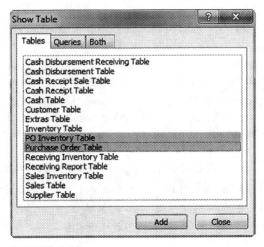

FIGURE 5-12

3. Create the relationship between **Purchase Order Table** and **PO Inventory Table** by dragging the primary key to the foreign key in the appropriate two tables. Recall that when you do this, the Edit Relationships window appears (Figure 5-13). Click on the **Enforce Referential Integrity** and **Cascade Update Related Fields** button.

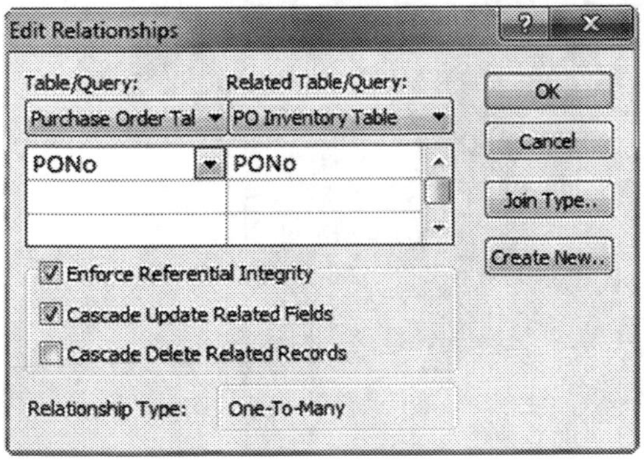

FIGURE 5-13

4. Create the other two necessary relationships.

5. Close the Relationships window and save the changes.

The Purchase Order Form

Now that the Relationships have been created, we are ready to begin creating the **Purchase Order Form**. As we found with the **Sales Form**, this form will require the use of several tables. We will need to be able to read from the **Supplier Table** to obtain supplier information and from the **Inventory Table** to obtain the description and cost of the items ordered. We will need to be able to write to the **Purchase Order Table** to enter the PO Number, date, and supplier information and to the **PO Inventory Table** to list the required Inventory IDs and quantities.

1. Click on the **Create** tab and choose the **Form Wizard** [Form Wizard] from the **Forms** section.

2. From the Tables/Queries pull-down menu (Figure 5-14), select the **Purchase Order Table** and select all three fields for inclusion in the form by clicking **>>**.

(**NOTE:** Before you select fields for inclusion from this table and from tables in the future, it is important to be sure that the last field is highlighted in the Selected Fields window. If it is not, the fields will be out of order when the form is created and you will have to rearrange them!)

3. Select the **Supplier Table** and select **SupplierName** for inclusion in the form.

4. Select the **PO Inventory Table** and, as before, select **InventoryID** and **POQuantityOrdered** for inclusion.

5. Select **Inventory Table** and select **InventoryDescription** and **InventoryCost** for inclusion in the form.

6. Click the **Next** button. The Form Wizard automatically suggests a layout for the **Purchase Order Form** (containing fields from the **Purchase Order Table** and the **Supplier Table**) with a subform (containing the fields from the **PO Inventory Table** and the **Inventory Table**).

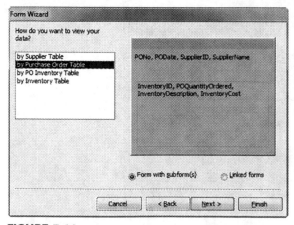

FIGURE 5-14

Accept the layout by clicking the **Next** button.

7. Select the Tabular layout for the subform in the next window and click **Next**. Select a style for your form and click **Next**. Change the name of the form to **Purchase Order Form** (leave the name of the subform alone). Click on **Modify the form's design**. Click on **Finish**.

8. Delete the label for the **SupplierName** field. Drag the Text Box for **SupplierName** so that it is opposite the **SupplierID** Text Box (Figure 5-15).

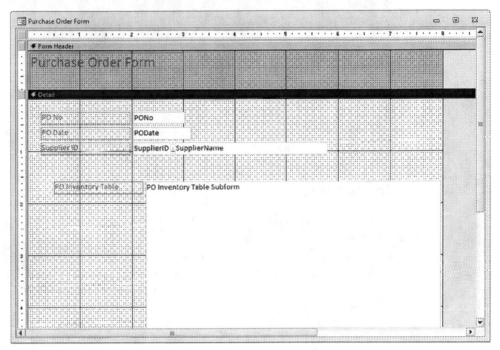

FIGURE 5-15

9. We want Supplier Name to automatically appear when the user types a Supplier ID into the Purchase Order Form. Recall from Chapter 4 that this provides us with closed-loop verification. Therefore, you should format the **SupplierName** so that the user cannot change the data that is entered in this field in the same manner as we protected the customer fields in the **Sales Form** in Chapter 4.

10. Right-click on the **SupplierName** Text Box and select Properties. Click on the **Data** tab and scroll down to the Enabled line. Change it to No. Scroll to the Locked line and change it to Yes. Click on the **Other** tab and click on **Tab Stop** and change it to No.

11. Click on the **Format** tab and click on **Back Color**. Click on the **Build** button and choose a color that will blend with the style of the form you choose. Click on **Border Style** and select Transparent from the pull-down menu. Close the Properties window.

12. We also want the Purchase Orders to remain in numerical order. Click on the **Form Selector** button between the two rulers on the Purchase Order form. Click on the **Data** tab and then click on the **Build** button on the **Record Source** property. Use the pull-down menu on the **Sort** property and change it to **Ascending** (Figure 5-16).

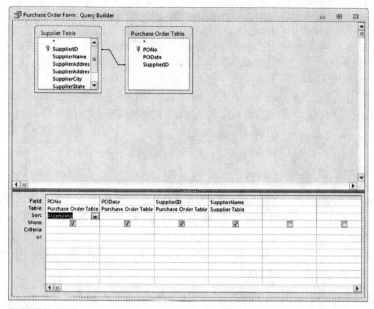

FIGURE 5-16

13. The subform also needs to be modified. First, click on the subform label and delete it.

14. We need to stretch it out to see the entire form. Click on the subform so that the handles appear. Drag the left side of the subform to the left side of the main form. Drag the right side of the subform to the right side of the main form (Figure 5-17).

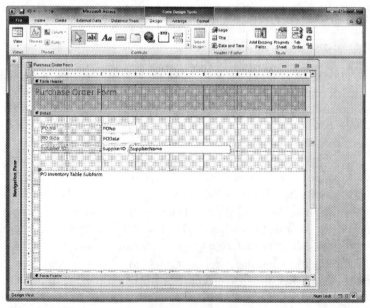

FIGURE 5-17

15. Double-click on the edge of the subform to open up the subform itself (Figure 5-18).

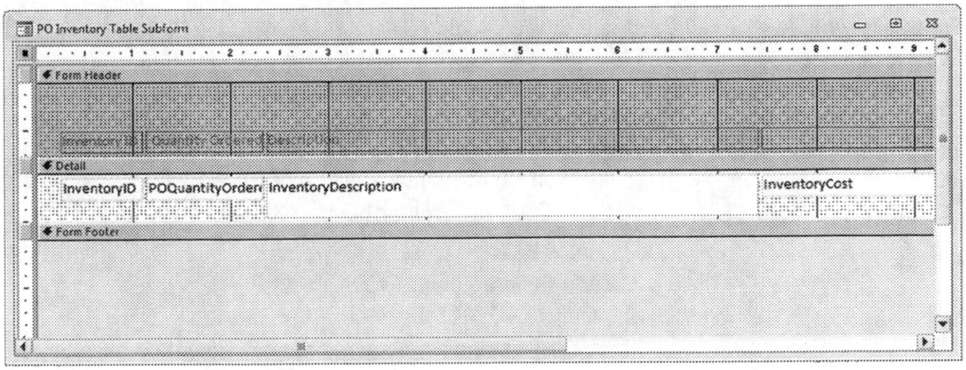

FIGURE 5-18

16. Scroll to the right of the subform and shrink the size of the **InventoryCost** Text Box and Label. Examine the label for **InventoryCost**. Notice that it is right justified. Click on the Align Left ▤ to left justify this label.

17. If necessary, shrink the width of the **InventoryDescription** field and label and move the **InventoryCost** field to the left. Just as we did not want the users to change the customer's information in the main portion of the **Purchase Order Form,** we do not want them to change the **InventoryDescription** or the **InventoryCost** in the subform. Change the properties on these two fields so that the user cannot enter or change anything.

18. Shrink the size of the form (Figure 5-19).

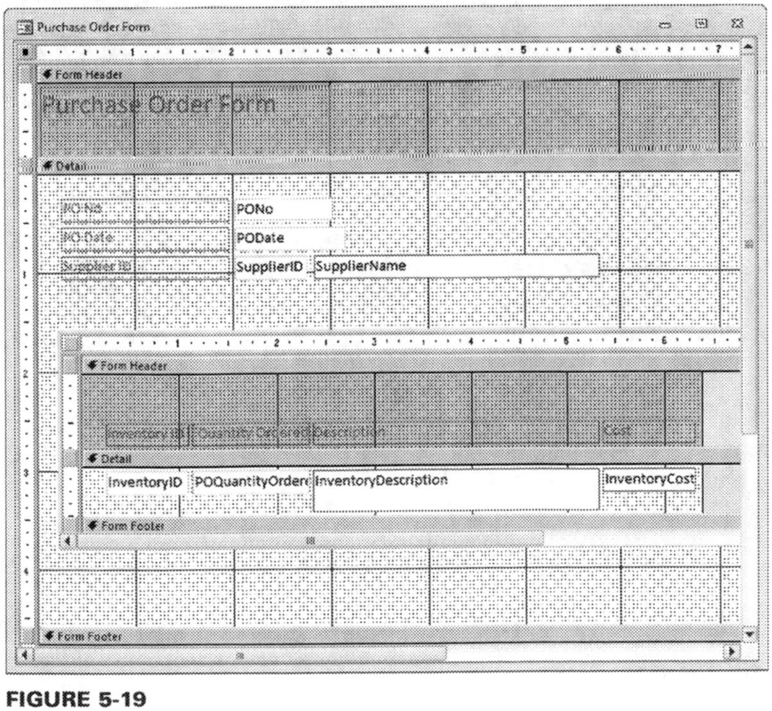

FIGURE 5-19

19. Save and close your form at this time.

20. Enter the following Purchase Orders at this time (Figure 5-20).

- PO No. 1000
  Vendor: SeaFoam (SEA100)
  Date: 10/15/2012
  Inventory Ordered:
  > 40 Egotists blanks (EG0000)
  > 25 King Creator blanks (KC0000)

- PO No. 1001
  Vendor: Clarke Foam (CLA132)
  Date: 10/18/2012
  Inventory Ordered:
  > 20 Imposer blanks (IM0000)
  > 20 Nice Devil blanks (ND0000)

- PO No. 1002
  Vendor: Clarke (CLA132)
  Date: 10/22/2012
  Inventory Ordered:
  > 15 Imposer blanks (IM0000)
  > 10 King Creator blanks (KC0000)

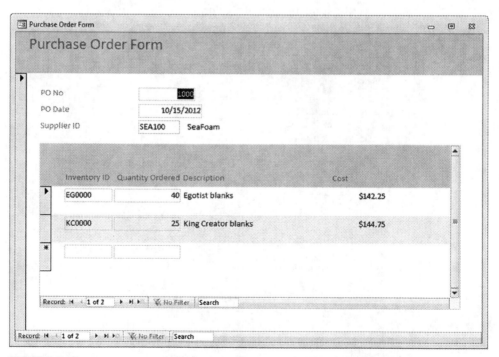

FIGURE 5-20

The Purchase Order Report

The Purchase Order we have created is an online form and is for internal purposes only. Just as with the Sales Invoice, we need to create a Purchase Order that we can mail to our suppliers. This requires the use of the Report object.

1. Click on the **Create** tab. Click on the **Report Wizard** ⟨ Report Wizard ⟩ icon in Reports section.

2. Select **Purchase Order Table** from the **Tables/Queries** pull-down menu (Figure 5-21). Select all the fields for inclusion by clicking on the ⟨ **>>** ⟩ button.

(**NOTE:** When performing these next steps, remember to place your cursor on the last field selected prior to selecting fields from the next table to ensure that the fields will be in the correct order in the **Purchase Order Report**.)

3. Select the **Supplier Table** and select all fields for inclusion. Return the **SupplierTable.SupplierID** field and the **SupplierPhone** field to the Available Fields window.

4. Select the **PO Inventory Table** and select **InventoryID** and **POQuantityOrdered** fields for inclusion.

5. Select the **Inventory Table** and select the **InventoryDescription** and **InventoryCost** fields for inclusion.

6. Click on **Next**. Accept the layout for the report design presented by the Report Wizard by clicking **Next** (Figure 5-22).

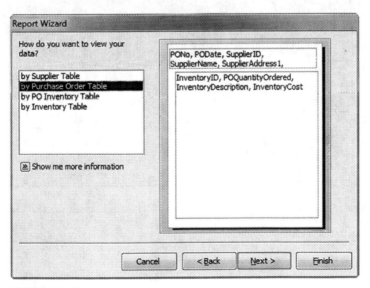

FIGURE 5-21

7. We do not need to add any additional groupings. Click on **Next**. Select **InventoryID** in the sort order combo box and click on **Next** (Figure 5-22).

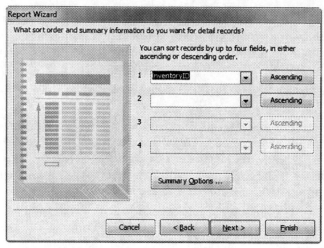

FIGURE 5-22

8. Choose a layout for the report and click on **Next**. (Note that we have chosen Outline for our layout.)

9. Change the report title to **Purchase Order Report** and click on **Modify the report's design** (Figure 5-23). Click **Finish**.

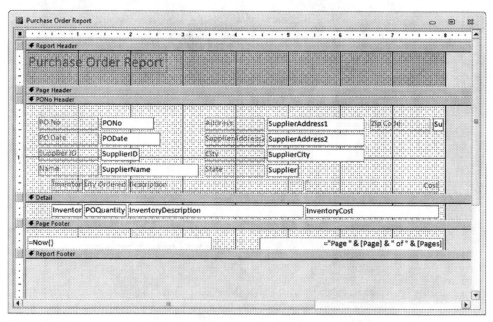

FIGURE 5-23

10. Drag the top of the Detail section bar down to make room in the PONo Header section. Drag all the fields in the Detail section down to meet the Detail section bar (Figure 5-24).

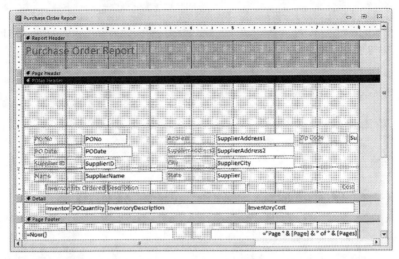

FIGURE 5-24

11. Drag the label from the Report Header section to the PONo Header section. Change the label from **Purchase Order Report** to **Purchase Order**.

12. Right click mouse and click **Page Header/Footer** to deselect it. When asked if you want to delete the section and all the controls in them, click **Yes** (Figure 5-25).

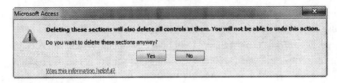

FIGURE 5-25

13. Deselect **Report Header/Footer** in the same manner (Figure 5-26).

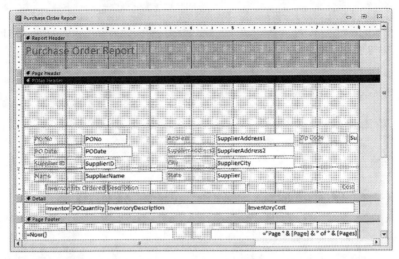

FIGURE 5-26

14. Right-click on the Form Selector (the box between the two rulers) and select Properties. Click on the **All** tab and click on the Build [⋯] button in the Record Source property to invoke the Query Builder (Figure 5-27).

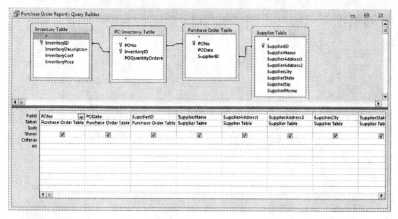

FIGURE 5-27

15. We want to make a composite address for the supplier, as we did for the customer. Scroll to the right in the design grid until you find an empty field. Place your cursor in the Field property and click on the **Builder** ⚒ Builder icon. In the upper portion of the Expression Window (Figure 5-28), type **SupplierCompAddress:**. Click on the Chapter 5 database and then double-click on **Tables** in lower left side of the Expression window. Click on the **Supplier Table**. Double-click on **SupplierCity**; click on **&**; type "**,**" (typed as an open quotation, comma, space, close quotation); click on **&**; double-click on **SupplierState**; click on **&**; type " " (typed as an open quotation, three spaces, close quotation); click on **&**; and double-click on **SupplierZip**. Remove the **<<Expr>>** that was automatically inserted just after the **SupplierCompAddress** field name from the expression. Click **OK**.

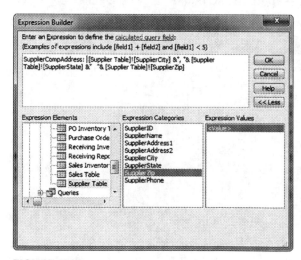

FIGURE 5-28

16. We also want to be able to extend to cost of the inventory ordered. Place your cursor in the next Field property and click on the Builder 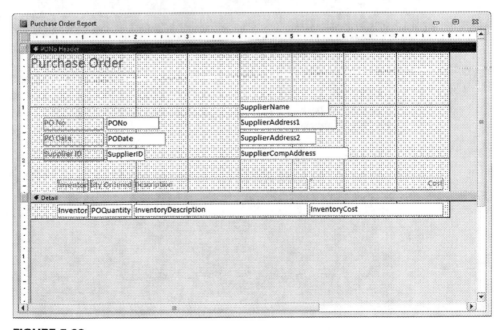 icon. Type **Extension:** in the upper window and click on the Chapter 5 database once more in lower left side of the Expression window. Double-click on the **Tables** and click on the **PO Inventory Table**. Double-click on **POQuantityOrdered**. Click on *****; double-click on the **Inventory Table** and double-click on **InventoryCost**. Remove the **<<Expr>>** that was automatically inserted just after the **Extension** field name from the expression (and any other **<<Expr>>** that may have appeared in your expression). Click **OK**.

17. Click on the **Run** ! icon. Close and save the query by clicking the X in the upper right corner. Close the Property window.

18. Delete the **SupplierCity**, **SupplierState**, and **SupplierZip** Text Boxes and Labels from the **Purchase Order Report**.

19. Delete the Labels for the **SupplierAddress1** and **SupplierAddress2** fields and drag the Text Boxes down to make room for the **SupplierName** (see Figure 5-29).

20. Delete the Label for the **SupplierName** field and drag the Text Box above the **SupplierAddress1** field.

21. Click on the **Add Existing Fields** icon under the **Design** main menu and drag the **SupplierCompAddress** to the PONo Header section, below the **SupplierAddress2** field. Delete the Label.

22. Format the **SupplierCompAddress** field so that the Border Style is Transparent.

23. Adjust the field lengths for the address fields.

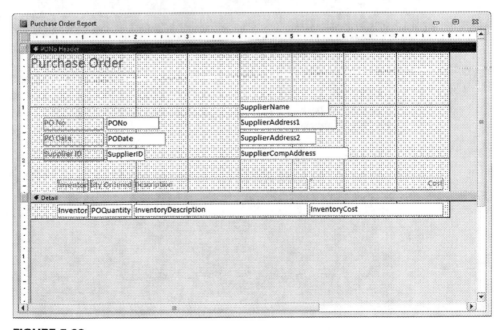

FIGURE 5-29

24. Now we need to look at the remainder of the Detail section. Make sure that all of the data are clearly visible. In the layout we have chosen, for example, many of the labels are truncated and the cost label needs to be realigned so that it is left-justified. Click on the **Cost** field. Click on the **Format** tab and click on the **Align Left** icon. Shrink the width of the **Cost** label and field.

25. Examine the layout for your report and make the necessary adjustments to make the report more user-friendly. Shrink the width of the **Description** label and field and move the **Cost** label and field to the left (Figure 5-30).

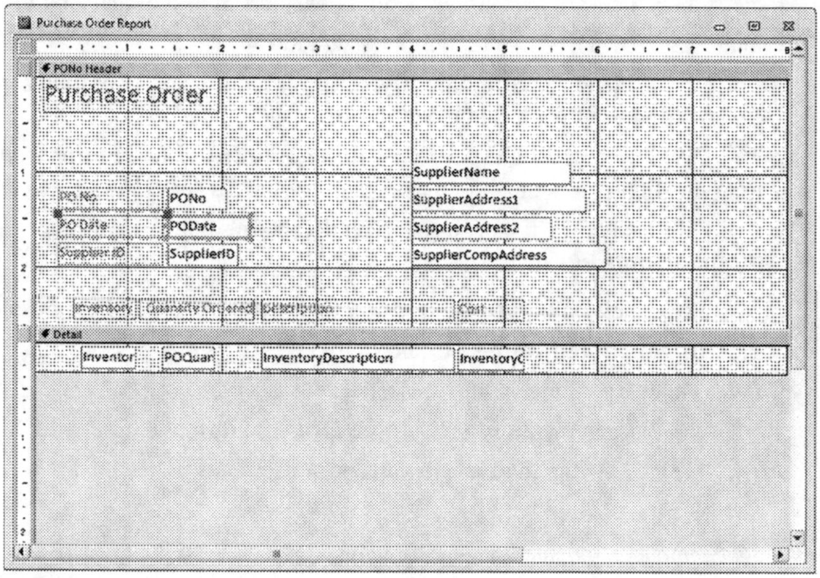

FIGURE 5-30

26. Click on **Add Existing Fields**. Add the **Extension** field next to the **Cost** field. (See Figure 5-31.) Right-click on the **Extension** field and click on Properties. Change the **Format** property to Currency. Change the **Border Style** to Transparent. Close the Properties window.

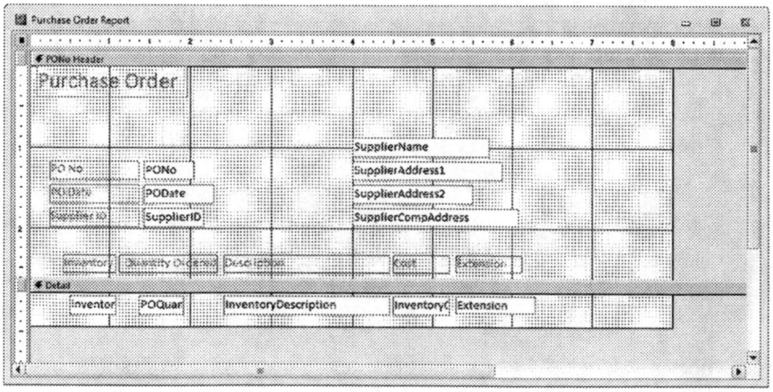

FIGURE 5-31

27. We also need to add Tragg's name, address, and phone number (provided to you at the beginning of this chapter), identifying the sender of the Purchase Order to the supplier. We do this by clicking on the Label *Aa* icon and typing in the necessary information. Note that you can only use one font size in one Label Box. We typically see the company name larger than the address information. To use varying font sizes so that you can make the company name larger than the address information, you will need to make two Label Boxes. When entering the address information, hold down the shift key and hit enter to add a line for the city, state, and zip information, etc. (See Figure 5-32.)

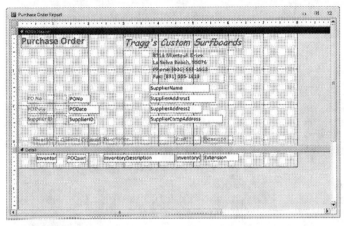

FIGURE 5-32

28. Finally, we need to sum the **Extension** field to arrive at a total for the **Purchase Order Report**. Similar to what we did for the **Sales Invoice Report**, this requires the addition of a PONo Footer. Click on the **Group & Sort** icon under the Design tab. (See Figure 5-33.)

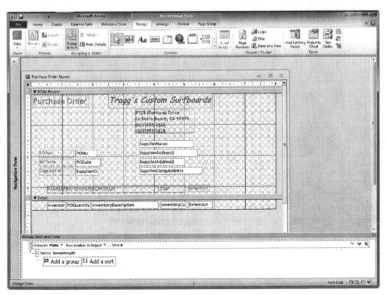

FIGURE 5-33

29. Click **More** More ► icon and change the **Without a Footer Section** to **With a Footer Section** and change the **Do not Keep Whole Group Together on One Page** to **Keep Whole Group Together on One Page**. (See Figure 5-34.) Close the **Group, Sort, and Total** window.

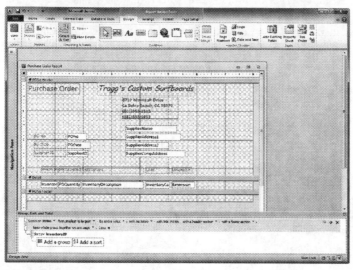

FIGURE 5-34

30. Click on the Text Box ab icon. In the PONo Footer Section, draw a Text Box under the **Extension** field for the **ExtensionTotal** field. (See Figure 5-35.) Right-click on the Text Box and click on Properties. Under the **Data** tab, click on the **Control Source** property and type **= Sum([Extension])**. Click on the **Format** tab and use the pull-down menu next to the **Format** property to select Currency. Change the **Border Style** to Transparent.

31. Change the caption for the label for the Text Box to **Purchase Order Total**.

32. Close the window.

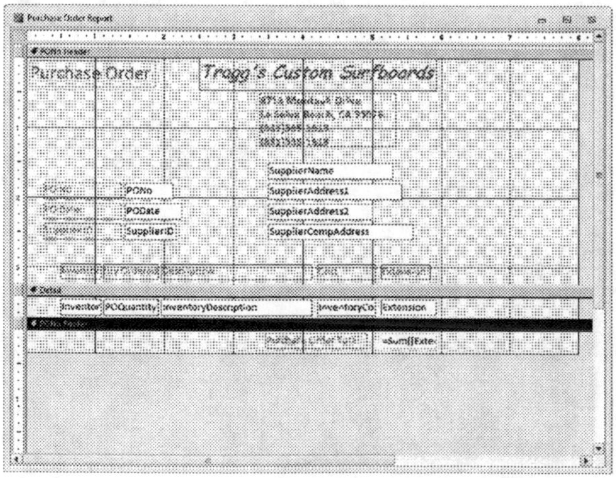

FIGURE 5-35

33. To avoid more than one **Purchase Order** printing on a single page, right-click on the PONo Footer and click on **Properties**. Under the Format tab, change the Force New Page property to After Section. (See Figure 5-36.) Close the Properties window.

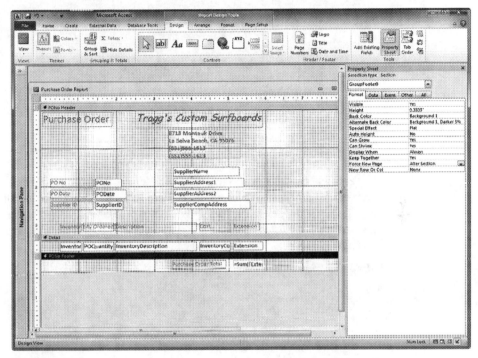

FIGURE 5-36

34. Make sure that all of your fields stay within the appropriate margins.

35. Close and save the **Purchase Order Report**.

The Receiving Report Form

Once the goods are ordered, we need to record their receipt upon delivery to the company. We do this through the creation of another form. Note that, while the Receiving Report is called a "Report," we do not have to create a *Report* in *Access* since the Receiving Report is an internal form.

1. Begin by opening the Relationships Relationships window. Click on the Show Table Show Table icon and add the **Receiving Report Table** and the **Receiving Inventory Table** to the Relationships window.

2. Create the required links based on the REA Diagram provided for you in Figure 5-1 and the table structure that followed. Enforce referential integrities where necessary. Close and save your changes to the Relationships window. (See Figure 5-37.)

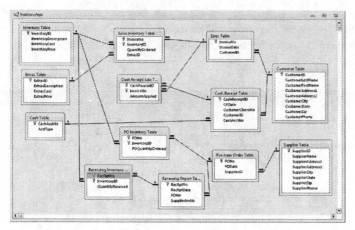

FIGURE 5-37

3. Click on the **Form Wizard** [Form Wizard] icon in the **Forms** section under the **Create** tab (Figure 5-38). Select the **Receiving Report Table** from the pull-down menu and select all the fields. Select the **Receiving Inventory Table** and select the **InventoryID** and **QuantityReceived** fields. Select the **Inventory Table** and select the **InventoryDescription** field. Click **Next**.

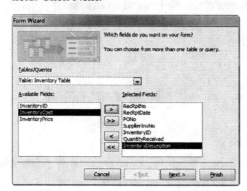

FIGURE 5-38

4. Accept the view by Receiving Report Table (Figure 5-39) and click **Next**.

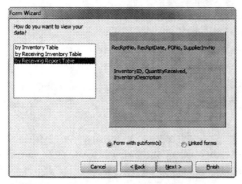

FIGURE 5-39

5. Click on **Tabular** for the layout in the next window and click on **Next**. Change the title of the form to **Receiving Report Form** and click on **Modify the form's design**. Click on **Finish**.

6. Delete the **Receiving Inventory Table Subform** label and stretch the subform to the left.

7. It would be beneficial if the users had the Supplier's name on the **Receiving Report Table**. To provide this, we have to have access to the **Supplier Table**. Right-click on the Form Selector (between the two rulers) and select Properties. Click on the **Data** tab. Click on the **Build** button for the **Record Source** of the form and invoke the **Query Builder**.

8. Click on the **Show Table** icon and add the **Supplier Table** (Figure 5-40). Notice that there is no relationship between the **Receiving Report Table** and the **Supplier Table**.

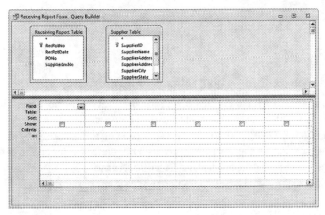

FIGURE 5-40

9. As a result, we will not be able to add the **SupplierName** to the form. We need to create a link between the two tables first. Think about what table will provide a link between these two tables. The **Purchase Order Table** satisfies this requirement. Add the **Purchase Order Table** and notice that the relationships automatically appear between the three tables (Figure 5-41).

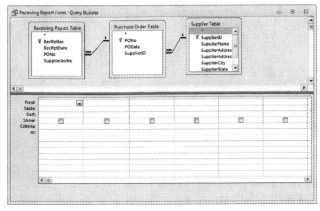

FIGURE 5-41

10. Drag all the fields from the **Receiving Report Table** to the first four fields of the design grids. Drag the **SupplierID** field from the **Purchase Order Table** to the fifth field. Drag the **SupplierName** from the **Supplier Table** to the sixth field (Figure 5-42).

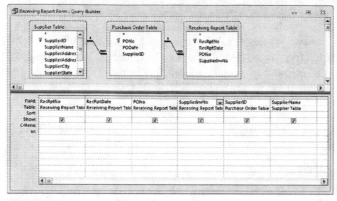

FIGURE 5-42

11. Click on the **Run** ! icon. Close and save the query. Close the Properties window.

12. Now that we have created a relationship between the **Receiving Report Table** and the **Supplier Table**, we can add the **SupplierName**. Click on the **Add Existing Fields** [...] icon under the Design main menu. Drag the **SupplierName** field to the upper right side of Detail section of the form (Figure 5-43). Delete the label and stretch out the field to be sure there is enough room for the **SupplierName**.

13. Move the **SupplierInvNo** field below the **SupplierName**.

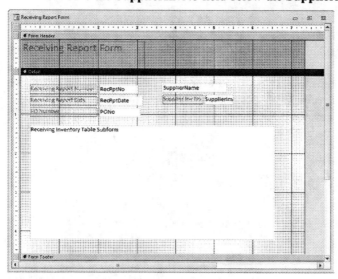

FIGURE 5-43

14. Click on the subform and open it.

15. Shrink the width of the InventoryDescription field and label. Exchange the positions of the **QuantityReceived** field and the **InventoryDescription** field (Figure 5-44).

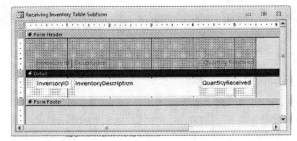

FIGURE 5-44

16. Right click on **InventoryDescription** and select Properties. Under the **Data** tab, change the Enable and Locked properties to keep users from changing the description field. Under the Other tab, change the Tab Stop field to No. Under the Format tab, change the Border Style to Transparent. Close the Properties window.

17. Close and save the subform. Close and save the form.

18. Receive the Purchase Orders created in the previous exercise, as follows:

- PO No. 1001 was received on 10/24/2012 (all items were received)
    Vendor: SeaFoam (SEA100)
    Supplier Inv No. 87462
    Inventory Ordered:
        40 Egotists blanks (EG0000)
        25 King Creator blanks (KC0000)

- PO No. 1001 was received on 10/26/2012 (all items were received)
    Vendor: Clarke Foam (CLA132)
    Supplier Inv No 9475
    Inventory Ordered:
        20 Imposer blanks (IM0000)
        20 Nice Devil blanks (ND0000)

- PO No. 1002 was received on 10/31/2012 (all items were received)
    Vendor: Clarke (CLA132)
    Supplier Inv No 9589
    Inventory Ordered:
        15 Imposer blanks (IM0000)
        10 King Creator blanks (KC0000)

Multi-step Queries

We created some simple queries in the Sales/Collection Business Process. We can create more complex queries to obtain more detailed information from the database, however. For example, Dan Tragg keeps close watch on his accounts payable and wishes to obtain the outstanding payable amount at the end of each month. This query requires multiple steps.

1. Click on the **Query Design** under Create main menu. Click on the **Inventory Table**, hold down the **Ctrl** key, and click on the **Receiving Inventory Table** and the **Receiving Report Table** in the Show Table window, click **Add** and click **Close**.

2. Drag **RecRptDate** into the first column of the design grid. Click on the **Totals** Σ icon. Change the **Total** property for **RecRptDate** to **Where** and enter **<=[BSDate]** as the Criteria. We are using a wild card because this is a query that Dan Tragg uses every month. The criteria must be "**<=**" so that it includes all purchases up to and including the date that is provided when prompted.

3. Place your cursor in the Field property of the second column in the design grid and click on the **Builder** icon. Type **InventoryPurchased:** in the upper portion of the Expression Builder window. Click on the database on the left-hand side of the lower portion of the window to open it up and then click on Tables. Click on the **Receiving Inventory Table**. Double-click on **QuantityReceived** in the middle window in the lower portion of the Expression Builder. Type "*****". Click on **Inventory Table** and double-click on **InventoryCost**. Remove the **<<Expr>>** portion of the expression. (See Figure 5-45.)

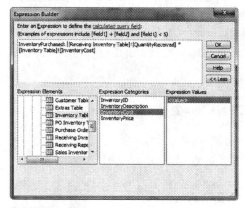

FIGURE 5-45

4. Click **OK** to close the Expression Builder window.

5. Click on the **Run** icon to see the results of the query, entering 10/31/2012 when prompted for a date (Figure 5-46).

FIGURE 5-46

6. Save the query as **Quantity Purchases Query**.

7. Click on the **Query Design** icon under the **Create** tab. We need to sum up the **InventoryPurchased** field we just created. Click on the Queries tab and double-click on the **Quantity Purchases Query** to add it. Close the Show Table window.

8. Drag the **InventoryPurchased** field to the first field in the design grid. Click on the Totals Σ icon. Change the Total property to Sum (Figure 5-47).

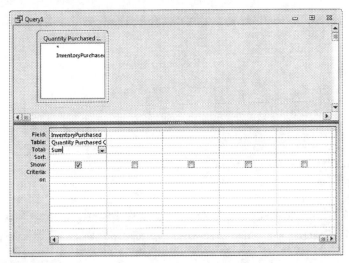

FIGURE 5-47

9. Click on the **Run** ! icon to see the results of the query, entering 10/31/2012 when prompted for a date.

10. Close and save the query as **Sum Purchases Query**.

11. Before we make our next query, we need to make sure that we have all of the relationships completed for all tables in our database. Open the **Relationships** window by clicking on the **Relationships** icon under the **Database Tools** tab. Add the **Cash Disbursement Receiving Table** and the **Cash Disbursement Table** and create the remaining relationships.

12. Click on **Query Design** under **Create** tab again. Click on **Cash Disbursement Table**, hold down the **Ctrl** key, and click on the **Cash Disbursement Receiving Table** in the Show Table window, click **Add** and click **Close**.

13. Drag **AmountApplied** from the **Cash Disbursement Receiving Table** to the first field in the design grid. Drag **CDDate** from the **Cash Disbursement Table** to the second field in the design grid.

14. Click on the Total Σ icon. Change the Total property for **AmountApplied** to **Sum**. Change the Total property for **CDDate** to **Where**. Enter "<=[BSDate]" as the Criteria property for **CDDate**.

15. Click on the **Run** ⚡ Run icon to see the results of the query, again entering 10/31/2012 when prompted for a date (Figure 5-48).

FIGURE 5-48

16. Close and save the query as **Total Cash Disbursements Query**.

17. There is one more step we have to make to arrive at outstanding accounts payable. Click on Query Design under Create main once more. However, this time we will click on the Queries tab. Notice that we have the two queries that we have just created listed here. Click on the **Total Cash Disbursements Query**, hold down the **Ctrl** key, and click on the **Sum Purchases Query** in the Show Table window, click **Add** and click **Close**.

18. Drag **SumOfInventoryPurchased** into the first field of the design grid and **SumOfAmountApplied** into the second field of the design grid.

19. We need to create a field for the Accounts Payable calculation in the third field. Click on the **Field** property on the third field and click on the **Builder** ⚙ Builder icon.

20. It is possible (although not likely, unless we were at the beginning of the period) that we could have null values if there were no purchases during the period. *Access* cannot handle null values in a calculation. It returns a null value also. To deal with this possibility, we insert the "null-to-zero" or Nz function into every part of the expression in which there is a possibility of a null value. (Note that it must be applied to each part of the expression separately rather than to the overall expression or it will evaluate the entire expression for null values rather than each variable individually.)

In the upper portion of the window, type "**Accounts Payable: Nz(**". (See Figure 5-49.) In the lower left window, open the database and open the Queries folder. Open the **Sum Purchases Query**. Double-click on **SumOfInventoryPurchased** in the middle lower portion of the window to add it to the upper portion of the window. Type "**) - Nz(**". Click on **Total Cash Disbursements Query**. Double-click on **SumofAmountApplied** in the middle lower portion of the window to add it to the upper portion of the window. Type "**)**". If any **<<Expr>>** have appeared in your expression, be sure to remove them now. Click **OK**.

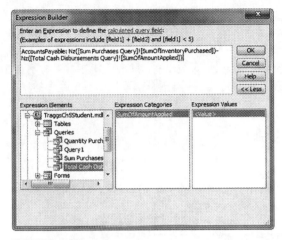

FIGURE 5-49

21. Remove the check mark from the **Show** property below the **SumOfInventoryPurchased** and **SumOfAmountApplied** fields (Figure 5-50). We do not need to have these amounts appear in the dynaset when we run the query. We are only interested in the Accounts Payable amount.

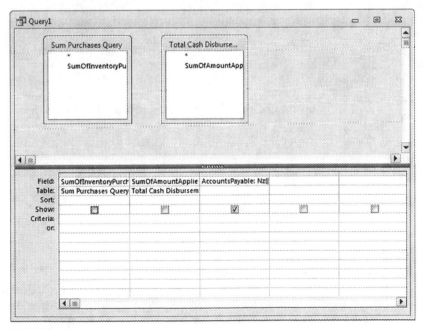

FIGURE 5-50

22. Right-click on the **AccountsPayable** field and click on Properties. Change the Format to Currency under the General Tab (Figure 5-51). Close the Properties window.

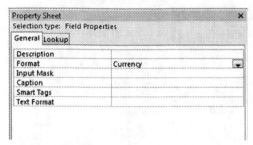

FIGURE 5-51

23. Click on the **Run** ⚡ icon to see the results of the query, again entering 10/31/2012 when prompted for a date (Figure 5-52).

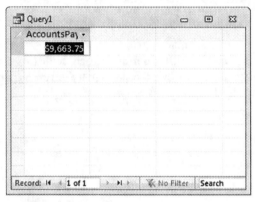

FIGURE 5-52

24. Close and save the query as **Accounts Payable Query**.

KEY TERMS

Acquisition/Payment business
process

Nz (null-to-zero) function
AutoNumber

QUESTIONS AND PROBLEMS FOR REVIEW

5.1 When we convert an REA diagram (a conceptual model) into a relational database,

(a) we should implement all relationships, regardless of maximum cardinalities, by posting the primary key of one entity into the other entity's table as a foreign key.

(b) we should implement a 1:1 (one-to-one) relationship with a separate table.

(c) we should implement a 1:N (one-to-many) relationship by posting the key of the many entity table into the one entity table.

(d) we should implement a 1:N (one-to-many) relationship by posting the key of the one entity table into the many entity table.

5.2 A company purchases unique (i.e. one-of-a-kind) inventory. The company purchases multiple items from their supplier as part of the same purchase to take advantage of lower shipping costs. The cardinality relationship (based on maximum cardinalities) between purchase and inventory are:
(a) 1:0.
(b) 1:N.
(c) 1:1.
(d) N:N.
(e) None of the above.

5.3 What is the purpose of the Nz (null-to-zero) function?
(a) The Nz function enables *Access* to treat null values as if they are zeroes for calculation purposes.
(b) The Nz function enables *Access* to treat non-null values as if they are null or zero for calculation purposes.
(c) The Nz function only affects *Access* calculations when there are both non-null and null values.
(d) The Nz function is only used for complex *Access* calculations.
(e) None of the above.

PROBLEMS

5.1 Dan Tragg has asked you to calculate the total purchases of each inventory item as of October 31, 2012. Create a query to do this. Your query should include the Inventory ID, quantity, unit cost and total dollar amount.

5.2 There are many items of inventory listed in the **Inventory Table**. It is hard to remember the item numbers when you are ordering goods. It might make the Purchase Order more user-friendly if we incorporated a pull-down menu for the **Purchase Order Form**. Revise the **Purchase Order Form** to make the **InventoryID** a combo box. In addition, we should add a total to the Purchase Order Cost column to provide information for internal decision makers.

5.3 Calculate the balance account payable by supplier as of October 31, 2012.

5.4 Create a **Cash Disbursements Form**. The form should include the Cash Disbursement ID, CD Date, Supplier ID, Supplier Name, Cash Account No, Receiving Report No, Amount Applied, and the total of the Amount Applied (with appropriate labels). Once the form has been created, pay PO No. 1001 on November 13, 2012.

5.5 Calculate the cash balance as of October 31, 2012.

CHAPTER 6

HUMAN RESOURCE BUSINESS PROCESS

INTRODUCTION

The Human Resource business process is often referred to as the payroll transaction cycle. The Human Resource process encompasses more than the disbursement of payments to employees for the labor services they provide, however. It also includes personnel functions, such as hiring, training, and firing employees. The instigation event in the Human Resource process is the labor requisition. The acquisition of labor is the economic increment event, while the payment for the labor is the economic decrement event (i.e., the cash disbursement).

To model the Human Resource business process in a database, we need to be able to create complex calculations. In addition, payroll contains very sensitive information that should not be readily available to most individuals in the organization. Therefore, it should be protected by internal controls that are not necessary in other cycles. After completing this chapter, you should be able to use Microsoft *Access* to:

- Create default values for fields.
- Create a customized data-entry form.
- Create a simple macro.
- Create a multi-step query.
- Create a union query.

HUMAN RESOURCE BUSINESS PROCESS OVERVIEW

Basic Concepts and Definitions

We once more look back to Figure 1-3 and see that the payroll cycle interfaces with the conversion cycle, the financing cycle, and the financial reporting system. By applying this to our framework of business processes, we can see that labor is acquired by a company through the Human Resource process. The Human Resource process provides labor to the Conversion process for the production of finished goods, which in turn delivers those goods to the Sales/Collection Process for sale and subsequent collection of cash. Note that in service organizations, labor may also be provided to the Revenue process (in which case, it is also an economic decrement event). Once the revenue is collected, it is made available to the Financing process and, in turn, is used to pay for the labor acquired by the Human Resource process. For this to happen, the Human Resource process must include at least one economic event that transfers in the labor (i.e., an increment event). This is the acceptance of the labor services. It must also include at least one economic event that transfers out the cash for wages and salaries (i.e., a decrement event). This is the payroll event, i.e., the payment for the labor services. The Human Resource process for all firms is similar regardless of whether the firm is engaged in manufacturing, in service, or in retail.

Tragg's Custom Surfboards

Additional Background Dan Tragg has gathered a small but dynamic and enthusiastic workforce in the company. Most of them have been with him since the company's inception. Dan is the President and Chief Executive Officer of the company. Casey Cameron, Dan's sister, is the company's Managing Director. Sara Tierno is the company's Marketing Director. Charlie Murray is the Production Supervisor. Miguel Santana is the Controller. They are all full-time, salaried employees. The remaining employees are also full-time but they are paid on an hourly basis. Brenda Chan, Nancy Wood, and John Walker comprise the Sales force. David Sinclair, Theresa Chung and Juan Santiago are the three full-time production employees. Edward Israel is the accounting clerk.

Model the Payroll Cycle Using REA Tragg's Human Resource process is relatively simple. If the company needs to hire new employees, Casey Cameron, the Managing Director, places an advertisement in the local newspapers. They also rely on referrals from their existing employees. Casey is responsible for interviewing all potential employees. If they have the appropriate qualifications, she then refers them to the appropriate supervisor (i.e., sales candidates to the Marketing Director, production candidates to the Production Supervisor, and accounting candidates to the Controller). She discusses the candidates with the appropriate supervisor and makes the final decision with regard to hiring the individual.

When an employee is hired, the accounting clerk enters his or her personnel information into the database. The sales force, production team, and accounting clerk are paid on an hourly basis. Tragg's pays all employees for holidays and pays the hourly staff time and a half for overtime. All employees are paid on the 15th and the last day of the month.

On payday (the 15th or the last day of the month or the first business day following that day), the supervisor for each department verifies the accuracy of each employee's timecard and inputs the hours for each into the database. One copy of the timecard is filed in the department and another is sent to the accounting department for filing. (It is important to note that this part of the process is not actually part of the payroll process but rather actually part of the conversion process and is not, therefore, described in Figure 6-1.)

The database automatically calculates payroll based upon the information that has been entered into it. The accounting clerk is responsible for verifying the gross pay, withholdings, and net pay dollar amounts that are calculated by the database and for printing the payroll checks.

There is a separate checking account for payroll. Payroll checks are approved by the Controller and are signed by Dan Tragg. This basic process is described in Figure 6-1.

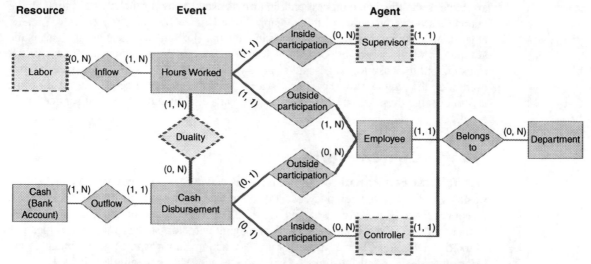

FIGURE 6-1 Basic REA Diagram for Tragg's Custom Surfboards Payroll Cycle

In order to create the payroll, however, there are several other "entities" involved. For example, it is necessary to reference the number of withholding allowances an individual has claimed and the withholding tables for tax calculation purposes. Therefore, we need to amend Figure 6-1 to include these additional reference tables (Figure 6-2).

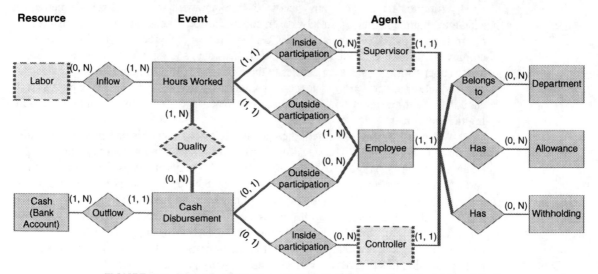

FIGURE 6-2 Amended REA Diagram for Tragg's Custom Surfboards Payroll Cycle

Create a Relational Database for Tragg's Following the REA Diagram

Tragg's table structure for the Human Resource Business Process can be represented as follows:

Cash Table (<u>CashAcctNo</u>, AcctType)

Department Table (<u>DeptNo</u>, DeptDescription)

Hours Worked Table (<u>EmployeeNo</u>, <u>PPEnded</u>, RegularTimeHours, OvertimeHours)

Employee Table (<u>EmployeeNo</u>, EmployeeLastName, EmployeeFirstName, EmployeeMiddleInitial, EmployeeSSNo, EmployeeAddress1, EmployeeAddress2, EmployeeCity, EmployeeState, EmployeeZip, EmployeePhone, DateOfBirth, MaritalStatus, <u>TaxBracket</u>, <u>AllowanceNo</u>, PayStatus, PayRate, EmployeeStartDate, <u>DeptNo</u>)

Withholding Table (<u>TaxBracket</u>, TaxRate, FWT, UpperLimit)

Allowance Table (<u>AllowanceNo</u>, AllowanceAmount)

Notice that we did not include the **Cash Disbursement Table** in our table structure because it has already been created in Chapter 5.

Tragg's Relational Database using Access We have created some of the tables for you in prior chapters and provided additional tables for you for this chapter. However, the Payroll Cycle contains a great deal of sensitive information. Therefore, there is an opportunity to implement controls and constraints as we build the tables in this cycle and we will start by building the **Employee Table**.

The Employee Table

The **Employee Table** holds data regarding the employee's personal information, the employee's job information, and the employee's payroll information.

1. Click on the **Create** tab and click on the **Table Design** icon.

2. The first field will be the **EmployeeNo**. We will have no need to perform any calculations on this field; therefore, set the Data Type to **Text**. (See Figure 6-3.) Click on the **Primary Key** ⚲ Primary Key icon to set the field as the primary key. Now move to the Field Properties and set the Field Size to **4**. The Caption should be **Employee No**. It is a **Required** field.

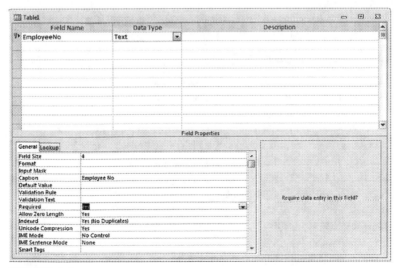

FIGURE 6-3

3. The Data Types for the following fields should all be set to **Text**. The second field is **EmployeeLastName**, the Field Size is 30, and the Caption should be **Last Name**. The third field is **EmployeeFirstName**, the Field Size is 20, and the Caption should be **First Name**.

4. The fourth field is **EmployeeMiddleInitial**, the Field Size is 1, and the Caption should be **Middle Initial**. We will use an Input Mask for this field to assist the users on input of the data. In the Input Mask property, type **>L**. This will ensure than the input is alphabetic and will convert any lower case input into upper case.

5. The fifth field is **EmployeeSSNo**, the Field Size is 11, and the Caption is **Social Security No**. We will again use an Input Mask for this field. However, this time we will use the Build 🔲 button next to the Input Mask property. When asked if you want to save the table, click **Yes** and name it as **Employee Table**. When the Input Mask Wizard window appears (Figure 6-4), select the Social Security Number option and click **Next**. Click **Next** in the following two windows to accept the input mask and the manner in which it is stored, and then click **Finish**.

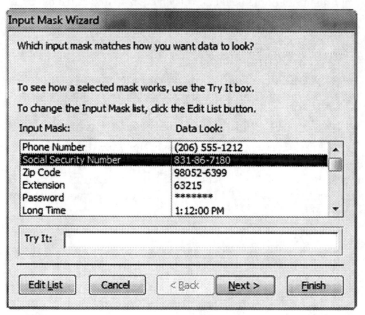

FIGURE 6-4

6. The sixth field is **EmployeeAddress1**, the Field Size is 35, and the Caption is **Address**. The seventh field is **EmployeeAddress2**, the Field Size is 10, and there is no Caption since this is the second line to the Address field. The eighth field is **EmployeeCity**, the Field Size is 25, and the Caption is **City**. The ninth field is **EmployeeState**, the Field Size is 2, and the Caption is **State**. We will again use an Input Mask for this field to assist the users on input of the data. In the Input Mask property, type **>LL**. As we saw with the **EmployeeMiddleInitial** field, this will ensure that the input is alphabetic and will convert any lower case input into upper case.

7. The tenth field is **EmployeeZip**, the Field Size is 10, and the Caption is **Zip Code**. We will again use an Input Mask for this field. However, this time we will use the

Build ⟦...⟧ button next to the Input Mask property to invoke the Input Mask Wizard. Use the Zip Code Input Mask as we did for the **Customer Table** and the **Supplier Table** (in Chapters 4 and 5). Complete the steps in the Input Mask Wizard.

8. The eleventh field is **EmployeePhone**, the Field Size is 14, and the Caption is **Phone Number**. Once again, click on the **Build** ⟦...⟧ button to invoke the Input Mask Wizard and select the Phone Number Input Mask. Complete the steps in the Input Mask Wizard.

9. The twelfth field is **DateOfBirth**. We will change the Data Type to Date/Time. Once again, click on the **Build** ⟦...⟧ button to invoke the Input Mask Wizard and select the **Short Date** input mask. Click on **Finish**. The Caption is **Date of Birth**.

10. The thirteenth field is **MaritalStatus**, the Field Size is 1, and the Caption is **Marital Status**. The Data Type is Text. We will use an Input Mask for this field to assist the users on input of the data. In the Input Mask property, type **>L**. Unless an employee declares his or her marital status to be married, by default the law considers them to be single. Therefore, we will set the Default Value at "S." We also want to ensure that no value other than **"M"** for Married or **"S"** for Single is entered in this field. Thus, we will set the Validation Rule as = **"S" Or "M"**. Finally, we want to include a Validation Text informing the user of the input requirements should he or she make an invalid entry in this field. Type **"Enter S for Single; M for Married"** in the Validation Text property (Figure 6-5).

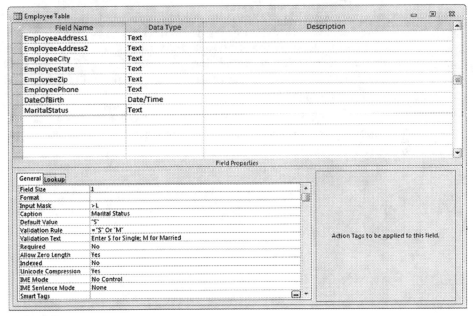

FIGURE 6-5

11. The fourteenth field is **TaxBracket**, the Data Type is Text, the Field Size is 2, and the Caption is **Tax Bracket**.

12. The fifteenth field is **AllowanceNo** and the Data Type is Number. The Field Size is **Byte** and the Decimal Places is set to **0** since the value for this field will always be a whole number. The Caption is **Allowance No**.

13. The sixteenth field is **PayStatus**, the Data Type is **Text**, the Field Size is **1**, and the Caption is **Pay Status**. Use the Input Mask property to assist the users on input of the data by typing **>L**. We want to ensure that no value other than "H" for Hourly or "S" for Salaried is entered in this field. Thus, we will set the Validation Rule as **= "H" Or "S"**. We also want to include a Validation Text informing the user of the input requirements should he or she make an invalid entry in this field. Type "**Enter H for Hourly; S for Salaried**" in the Validation Text property.

14. The seventeenth field is **HPayRate**, the Data Type is **Currency**, and the Format is **Currency**. Set the Decimal Places to **2** and the Caption to **Hourly Pay Rate**.

15. The eighteenth field is **SPayRate**, the Data Type is **Currency**, and the Format is **Currency**. Set the Decimal Places to **2** and the Caption to **Salaried Pay Rate**.

16. The nineteenth field is **EmployeeStartDate**. We will change the Data Type to Date/Time. Once again, click on the **Build** [...] button to invoke the Input Mask Wizard and select the **Short Date** input mask. Click on **Finish**. The Caption is **Start Date**.

17. The twentieth field is **DeptNo**, the Data Type is Text, the Field Size is 2, and the Caption is **Dept No**.

18. The last field is **JobTitle**, the Data Type is **Text**, the Field Size is 35, and the Caption is **Job Title**.

The Employee Form

Think about the fields that we created in the **Employee Table**. These fields fell into three categories: the employee's personal information, the employee's job information, and the employee's payroll information. As we design the **Employee Form**, we will keep those fields together in separate categories to make the form more user-friendly and to facilitate the input of data.

1. Click on the **Create** tab and click on the **Form Design** icon. (See Figure 6-6.) Click on the **Property Sheet** icon, be sure **Form** is in the **Selection type** window and click

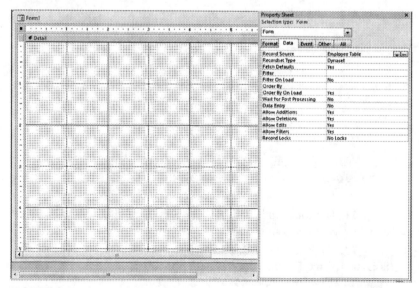

FIGURE 6-6

on the **Data** tab. Select **Employee Table** from the pull-down menu next to the **Record Source** property.

2. Click on the Build ![...] button. Click yes to invoke to Query Builder (Figure 6-7). Click on the Show Table ![icon] icon. Add all the fields to the query. Click on the Run icon, close and save the query.

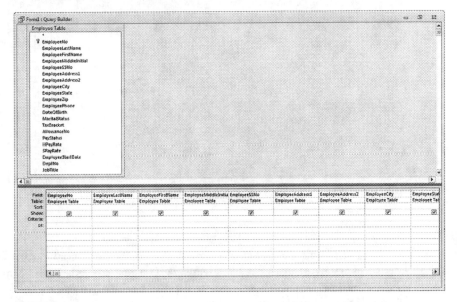

FIGURE 6-7

3. Click on the **Add Existing Fields** ![icon] icon. Notice that the Field List window contains all the **Employee Table** fields (Figure 6-8).

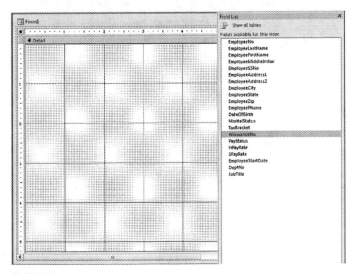

FIGURE 6-8

4. Click on **Design** tab and then click on the **Rectangle** [ ] icon in the **Controls** section. (Note: You may need to scroll down to find the **Rectangle** icon.) Starting in the upper left-hand corner of the form, drag a rectangle out approximately 3 inches wide and 3 ¹/₂ inches long (Figure 6-9).

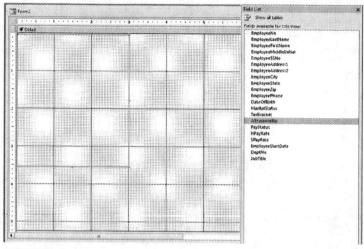

FIGURE 6-9

5. Click on the **Label** *Aa* icon in the Toolbox and draw a narrow rectangle for a label centered, at the top, of the rectangle you just created. Type "**Employee Personal Information**" in this label (Figure 6-10). Click on the **Home** tab. Click your cursor outside of this rectangle and then click the new label once to highlight it. Click on the **Bold** **B** icon in the **Home** tab and then click on the **Align Center** ☰ icon.

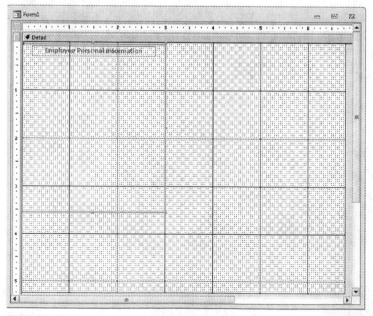

FIGURE 6-10

6. Click on the **Design** tab and click on the **Rectangle** icon again. Draw another rectangle beginning at approximately the 3 $^1/_2$ inch mark to approximately the 6 $^1/_2$ inch mark on the top ruler and down approximately 2 inches in length. Draw one more rectangle below that rectangle beginning at approximately 2 $^1/_2$ inch mark to the 7 inch mark on the top ruler and down to the 4 $^1/_2$ inch mark. Click on the **Label** icon and draw a label at the center top of the newly created rectangle. Type "**Employee Job Information**" in this label. Center it and make it bold as you did with the label in the first rectangle (see Step 6). Make a label for the second new rectangle. Type "**Employee Payroll Information**" in this label, center it and make it bold (Figure 6-11).

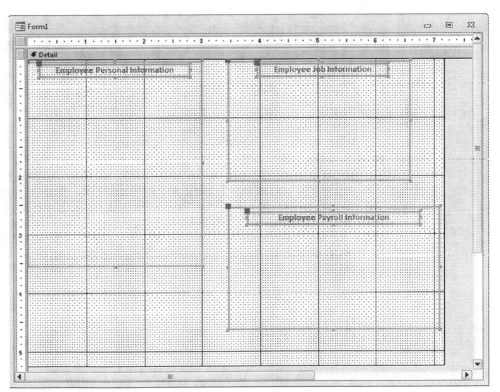

FIGURE 6-11

7. Now we will begin to populate the three categories we have created with the fields from the **Employee Table**. Click on the **Design** tab and click on the **Add Existing Fields** icon. Drag the following fields into the **Employee Personal Information** rectangle: **EmployeeNo**, **EmployeeFirstName**, **EmployeeMiddleInitial**, **Employee-LastName**, **EmployeeAddress1**, **EmployeeAddress2**, and **EmployeeCity**. Since **EmployeeState** and **EmployeeZip** are not long fields, we can place them next to each other. Drag them into the rectangle and place them next to each other. Drag **EmployeePhone** and **DataOfBirth** into the rectangle. Now that we have the fields that we want in this area, we need to clean this up and make it user-friendly (Figure 6-12).

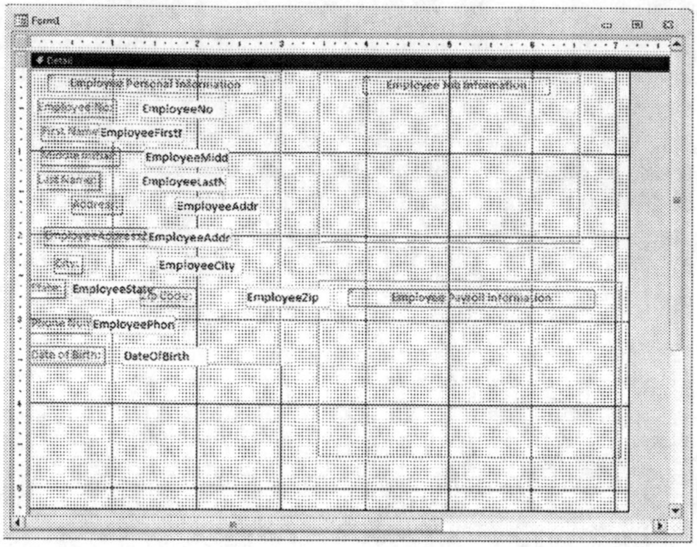

FIGURE 6-12

8. Stretch the **EmployeeNo** label to the left edge of the rectangle (Figure 6-13). Click on the Text Box and drag the left side of the Text Box to the right so that the label and the Text Box are next to each other but are not overlapping. The effect that you want to achieve here is to size the label so that it fits the amount of text inside it and then move the field (the Text Box) so that the left edge of the Text Box is next to the right edge of the label. As you will recall, the **EmployeeNo** field is 4 characters in length, so when you are sizing the Text Box, make sure you size it so that you are allowing space for a field that is approximately that large. Once you have done this, double-click on the label and delete the colon at the end of the label.

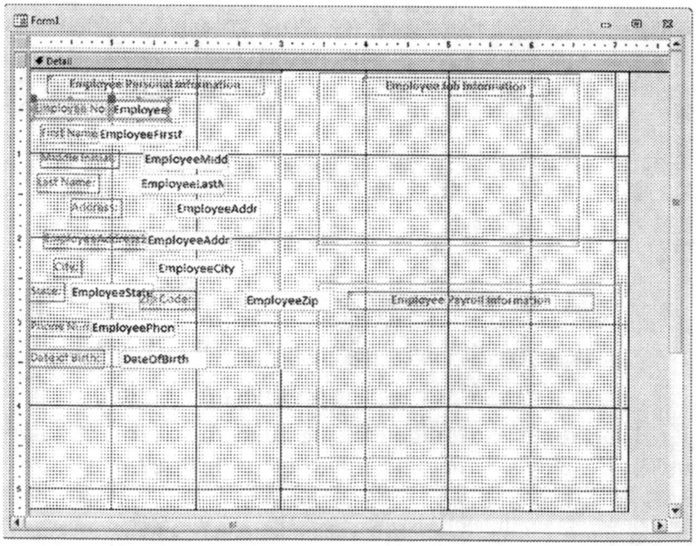

FIGURE 6-13

9. Align the label for **EmployeeFirstName** below the label for **EmployeeNo** but begin the Text box at approximately the 1-inch mark on the top ruler. Delete the colon from the label and stretch the label out to approximately the 2 $1/4$ inch mark. Do the same thing for **EmployeeMiddleInitial**, **EmployeeLastName**, **EmployeeAddress1**, **Employee-Address2**, and **EmployeeCity**. Delete the label for **EmployeeAddress2**. Go back and shrink the Text Box for **EmployeeMiddleInitial**. Remember that this field was created to accommodate one capital letter.

10. Align the label for **EmployeeState** below the other labels and shrink the Text Box. Remember that this field only needs to be large enough to accommodate two capital letters. Delete the colon in the label.

11. Move the **EmployeeZip** label and field next to the **EmployeeState** field. Adjust the length of the label and Text Box and delete the colon in the label.

12. Align the label for **PhoneNumber** below the other labels. Delete the colon from the label and stretch the Text Box out to the 2 $1/4$ inch mark.

13. Leave a small space before going on to the **DateOfBirth** field. Align the label for **DateOfBirth** below the other labels. Delete the colon from the label and stretch the Text Box out to accommodate the date (Figure 6-14).

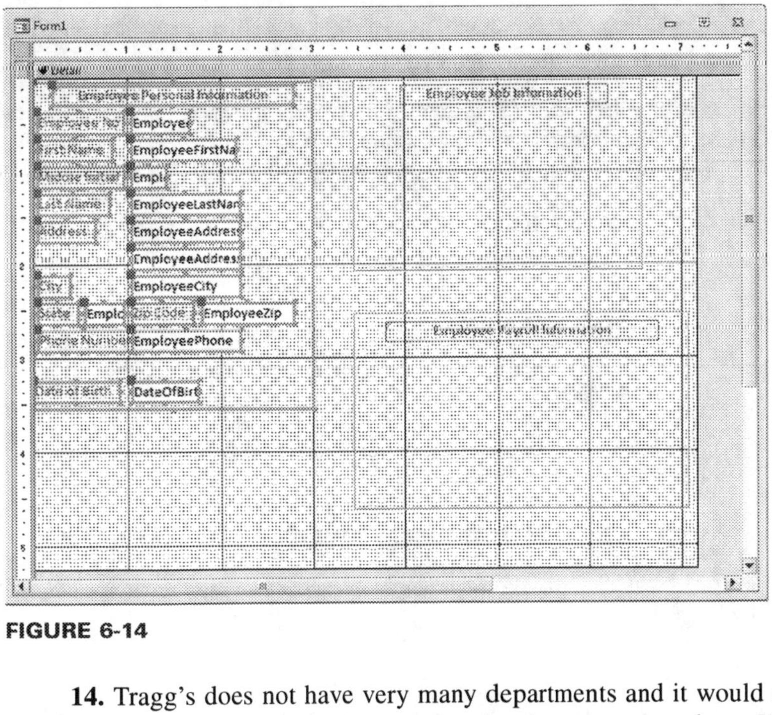

FIGURE 6-14

14. Tragg's does not have very many departments and it would not be very difficult for the accounting clerk to memorize the department numbers. However, it would make the form much more user-friendly and result in fewer input errors if the clerk could select the department name from a pull-down menu. Therefore, we will create a Combo Box for the **DeptNo** field. Click on the **Design** tab and then click on the **Combo Box** icon. Draw a rectangle below the heading label in the **Employee Job Information** rectangle (Figure 6-15).

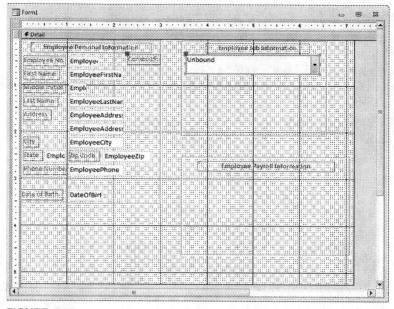

FIGURE 6-15

15. Since we created this form without the use of the Form Wizard, we don't have the use of other wizards. Therefore, we are going to enter values into the Combo Box Property Sheet ourselves. (See Figure 6-16.)

16. If the Property Sheet is not open for the Combo Box, highlight the Combo Box and click on the **Property Sheet** icon. Click on the **Row Source** property and click

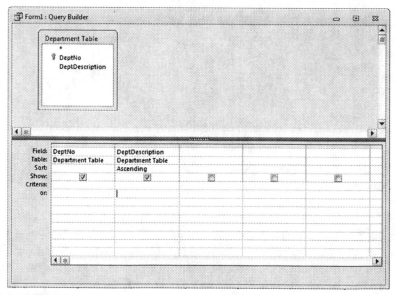

FIGURE 6-16

on the **Build** [···] button. The **Row Source** property tells the Combo Box where to go to obtain the data to be entered into the Combo Box. Add the **Department Table**. Drag the **DeptNo** to the first field and the **DeptDescription** to the second field. Select **Ascending** for the **Sort** property for the **DeptDescription** field. Click Run ⍋ and close and save the query.

Run

17. Click on the **Control Source** property. The **Control Source** property selects the field in which the data should be entered. We want the **DeptNo** from the **Department Table** (its primary key) to be entered into the **DeptNo** field in the **Employee Table** (where it is a foreign key). Therefore, select **DeptNo** from the pull-down menu (Figure 6-17).

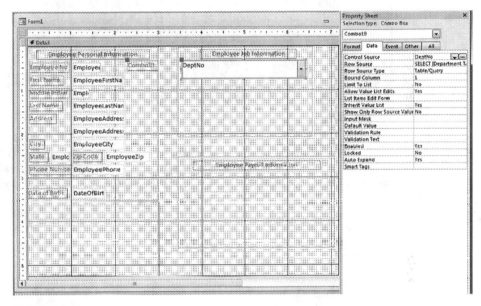

FIGURE 6-17

18. If you look at the form in Form View at this point, the Combo Box is not very helpful. It lists the **DeptNo** field rather than the **DeptDescription** field. Therefore, we still have some work to do with the Property Sheet.

19. Make sure that you are in the Property Sheet for the Combo Box, under the **Data** tab. (See Figure 6-18.) Notice that the **Limit to List** property is set to **No**. This property should be set to **Yes**. You don't want any additional fields added to the list. In addition, the **Allow Value List Edits** property is set to property is set to **Yes**. We do not want anyone to be able to change the values. Therefore, set this property to **No**.

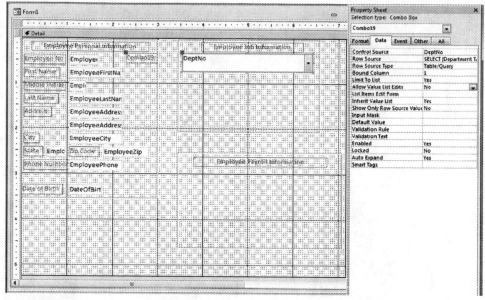

FIGURE 6-18

20. Click on the **Format** tab. Change the **Column Count** property to **2**. (See Figure 6-19.) We added two columns in the query (the first column was the **DeptNo** and the second was the **DeptDescription**). **DeptNo** is the primary key and, therefore, had to be part

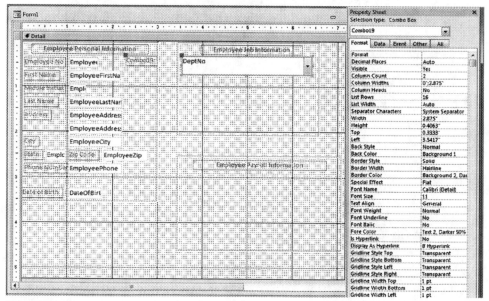

FIGURE 6-19

of the query but we don't need to have it appear in the Combo Box. Therefore, we can make the width of that column 0. Change the **Column Widths** property so that the first width is set to 0 and the second width is set equal to the **Width** property for the entire Combo Box (this property can be found lower in the Property Sheet). Shrink the Combo Box so that you have room for a label and create a label entitled "**Department**" for the field. (Note that, if the **Column Widths** property is not visible, you will have to click out of the **Format** tab for the change in the **Column Count** to take effect. In this case, click on the **Data** tab and then click on the **Format** tab again. Notice that you now have the ability to change the **Column Widths** property.)

21. Click on the **All** tab and enter **Department** in the **Name** property (Figure 6-20). Close the Property Sheet. Click on the label for the Combo Box and change it to **Department** and remove the colon and align the Combo Box and its label with the Employee Job Information rectangle.

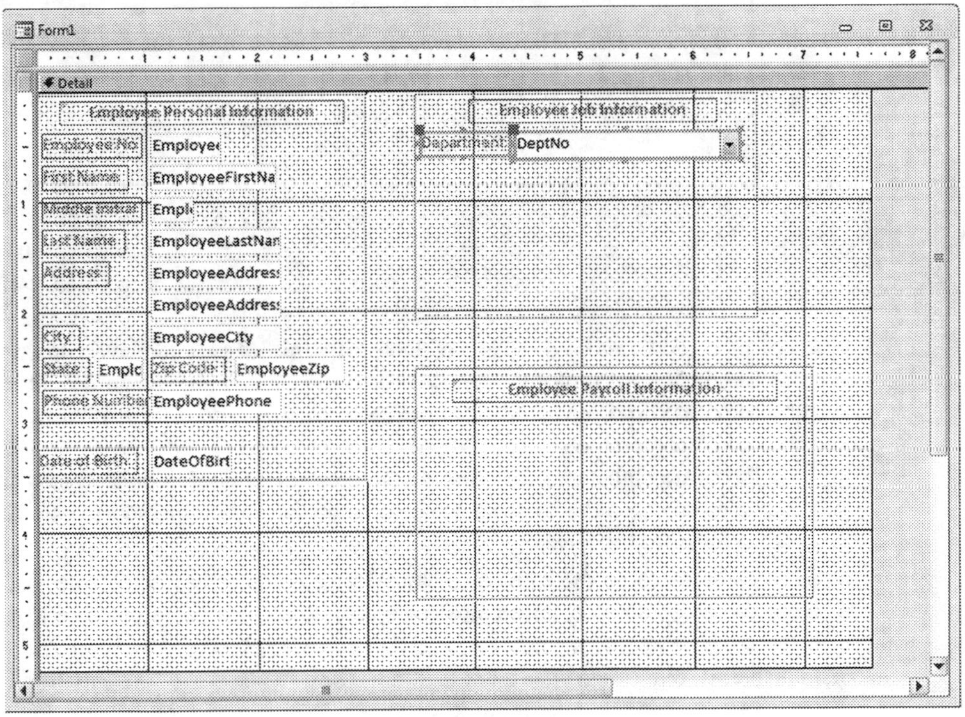

FIGURE 6-20

22. Click on the **Add Existing Fields** icon once more. Drag **JobTitle** and **EmployeeStartDate** into the **Employee Job Information** rectangle. Align the labels for **JobTitle** and **EmployeeStartDate** below the **Department** label. Delete the colon from the labels and adjust the Text Boxes out to accommodate the data. (See Figure 6-21.)

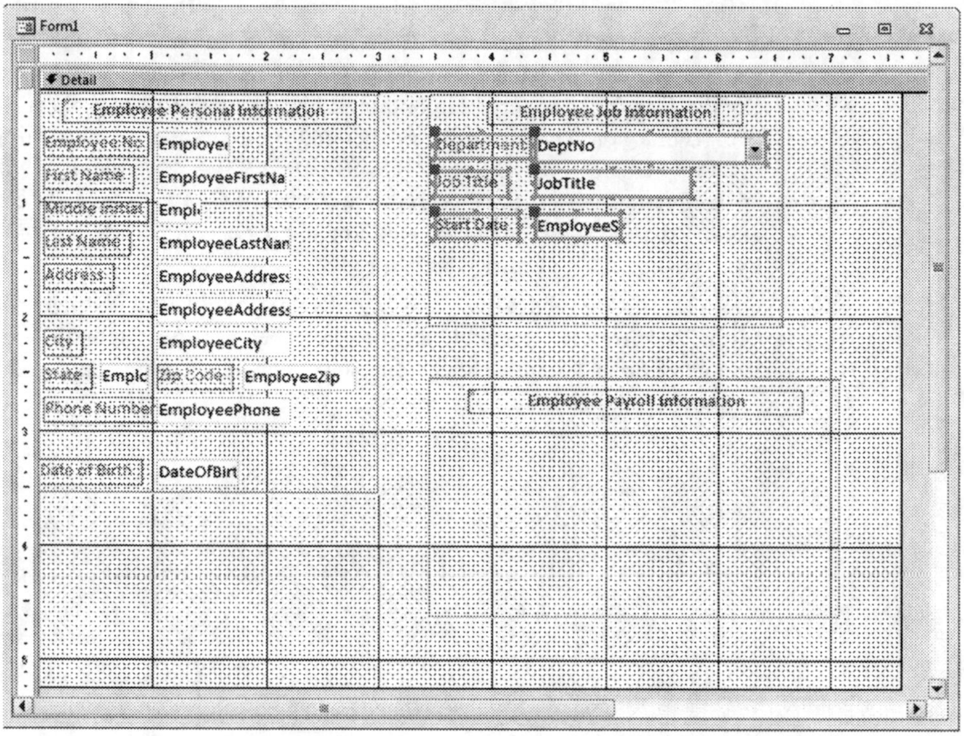

FIGURE 6-21

23. Drag the **EmployeeSSNo**, **MaritalStatus**, and **PayStatus** fields from the Field List into the Employee Payroll Information rectangle. Align the label and Text Box for **MaritalStatus** below the **EmployeeSSNo** label and Text Box. Since the **MaritalStatus** field only contains one character, you can shrink the size of the Text Box. Drag the **PayStatus** label and Text Box next to the **MaritalStatus** field. Again, since the **PayStatus** field only contains one character, you can also shrink the size of this Text Box. Delete the colon from the labels.

24. Drag the **AllowanceNo**, **HPayRate**, and **SPayRate** from the Field List into the Employee Payroll Information rectangle. Align the label and Text Box for **AllowanceNo** below the **MaritalStatus** label and Text Box. Align the label and Text Box for **HPayRate** below the **PayStatus** label and Text Box. Then align the label and the Text Box for **SPayRate** below the **HPayRate** label and Text Box. Delete the colon from the labels.

25. The **TaxBracket** field represents another area where we can make good use of the Combo Box. Take a moment and open the **Withholding Table**. Note that the primary key in this table is **TaxBracket**. Therefore, it is a foreign key in the **Employee Table** (just as the **DeptNo** was). We want to be able to determine the appropriate tax bracket for the employee based upon his or her marital status and pay rate. We can do this by referring to the **Withholding Table**. This table follows the 2011 IRS Tables for Percentage Method of Withholding. We will explain the calculation to determine federal withholding in more detail later when we create the query to calculate net pay. However, it is important to acquaint yourself now with the structure of the table. The table lists the schedule for married taxpayers first and then lists the schedule for single taxpayers. The second field, **TaxRate**, provides the tax rate to be applied on wages that do not exceed the bracketed amount. The last field, **UpperLimit**, provides the upper limit for the bracket. **FWT** is the amount to be added to the calculated tax to arrive at the total withholding.

The **UpperLimit** field is important to us here because it will help us to determine the **TaxBracket** to choose for each employee. By examining the table, we know that we can look at the **PayRate**, **MaritalStatus**, and **UpperLimit** fields and determine the **TaxBracket**. For example, if an employee is married and their **PayRate** is $3,750, his or her **TaxBracket** would be **M4**. It is important to note that, for purposes of simplification and illustration in this text, we have eliminated any possibility that an individual's allowances will reduce their wages to a lower **TaxBracket**. In reality, this tax calculation would involve far more steps than we include in this book. Our purpose is to provide you with a sense of the complexity involved in building the tables, forms, and queries in this cycle.

Close the **Withholding Table** now.

26. Click on the **Combo Box** ▦ icon and drag a rectangle below the **AllowanceNo** and pay rate fields.

27. From the Property Sheet for the Combo Box, click on the **Row Source** property and click on the **Build** ⟨...⟩ button. Select the **Withholding Table** from the **Show Table** window. Close the **Show Table** window.

28. Select **TaxBracket** and **UpperLimit** from the Available Fields window for inclusion. Click on the **Sort** property for the **Tax Bracket** field and select **Ascending** from the pull-down menu. Click the **Run** ❗ icon, close and save the query (Figure 6-22).

Employee Form : Query Builder			
Tax Bracket ▾	Upper Limit ▾		
M1	$329.00		
M2	$1,038.00		
M3	$3,204.00		
M4	$6,135.00		
M5	$9,175.00		
M6	$16,127.00		
S1	$88.00		
S2	$442.00		
S3	$1,525.00		
S4	$3,571.00		
S5	$7,354.00		
S6	$15,885.00		
*	$0.00		

Record: ◄ ◄ 1 of 12 ► ►► ►* 🚫 No Filter Search

FIGURE 6-22

29. Click on the **Control Source** property and select **Tax Bracket** from the pull-down menu.

30. We need to make changes to the properties in the Combo Box again. In the **Data** tab, change the **Limit to List** property to **Yes** and the **Allow Value List Edits** to **No**. In the **Format** tab, change the **Column Count** to **2**. Since both columns will be appearing in the Combo Box, the widths will adjust themselves. In the **All** tab, change the **Name** to **Tax Bracket**.

31. Delete the label for the Combo Box and create a new one by clicking on the Label icon **Aa** and drawing a rectangle above the Combo Box. Type **Tax Bracket** in this label (Figure 6-23). Click on the Label icon again and drag a rectangle above the remainder of the Combo Box. Type **Upper Limit** in this label.

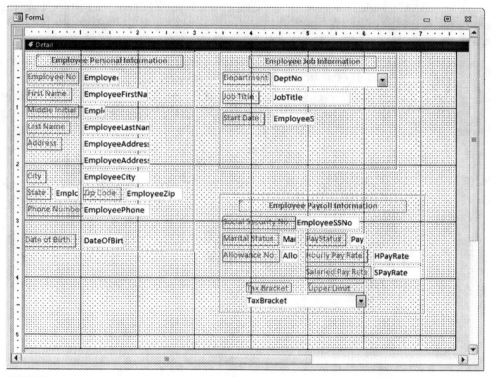

FIGURE 6-23

32. We now want to make it easier for users to navigate to the next record. We will create a button to do this. Click on the **Command** [xxxx] button in your Toolbox and draw a rectangle at the bottom of the form, outside and below the lower right-hand corner of the Employee Payroll Information rectangle. (See Figure 6-24.)

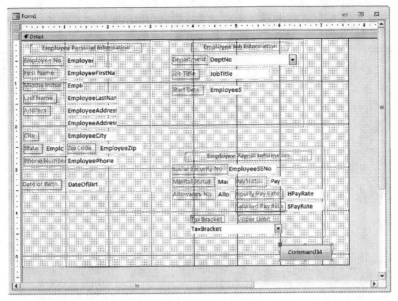

FIGURE 6-24

33. Right click on the **Command** button and select **Properties**. Click on the **Event** tab and click on the **Build** button next to the **On Click** property.

34. Select **Macro Builder** from the **Choose Builder** window and click **OK**. (See Figures 6-25 and 6-26.)

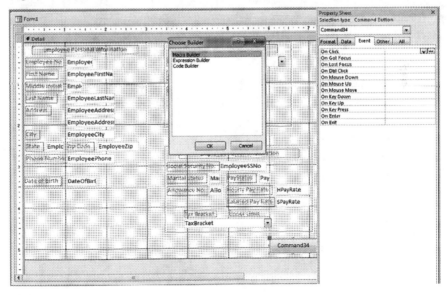

FIGURE 6-25

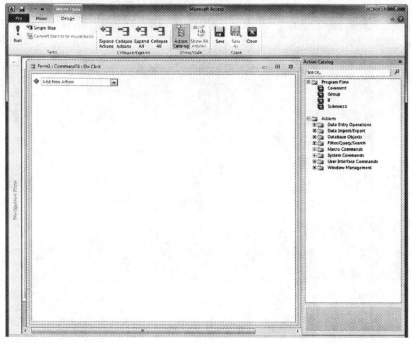

FIGURE 6-26

35. Using the pull-down menu next to **Add New Action** (or the Action Catalog under Database Objects), select **GoToRecord** (Figure 6-27).

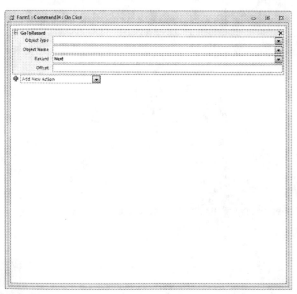

FIGURE 6-27

36. Select **GoToControl** as the second new action. (See Figure 6-28.) Enter **EmployeeNo** as the **Control Name**.

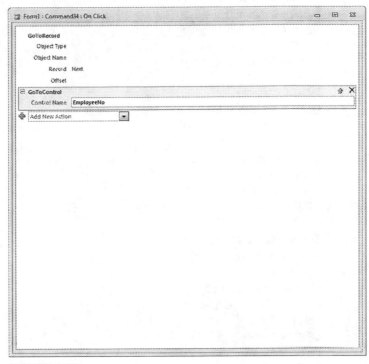

FIGURE 6-28

37. Close and save the changes to the macro. Click on the **All** tab for the **Command** button. Change the **Name** to **NextRecord** and the **Caption** to **Next Record**.

38. Close the Properties window.

39. Close and save the form as **Employee Form**.

40. Enter the following employee data at this time. We realize that this data entry is a tedious job. However, the data is necessary for the remainder of your practice to learn about the payroll process.

- Employee No 1001
  Dan W Tragg
  8713 Montauk Place
  La Selva Beach, CA 96076
  (831) 555-4374
  DOB 12/30/1967
  Dept: Administration
  Job Title: President
  Start Date: 9/1/1988
  SSN: 630-30-3003
  Marital Status: M
  Pay Status: S

Allowances: 2
Pay Rate: $5,500.00
Tax Bracket: M4

- Employee No 1002
Casey C Cameron
12773 Calma Court
La Selva Beach, CA 96076
(831) 555-4373
DOB 12/3/1970
Dept: Administration
Job Title: Managing Director
Start Date: 9/1/1988
SSN: 630-30-3113
Marital Status: S
Pay Status: S
Allowances: 0
Pay Rate: $4,000.00
Tax Bracket: S4

- Employee No 1003
Sara K Tierno
8713 Montauk Place
La Selva Beach, CA 96076
(831) 555-4374
DOB 8/15/1968
Dept: Marketing and Sales
Job Title: Marketing Director
Start Date: 10/19/1990
SSN: 661-77-2937
Marital Status: M
Pay Status: S
Allowances: 1
Pay Rate: $3,500.00
Tax Bracket: M3

- Employee No 1004
Nancy C Wood
22 Greenhill Lane
Santa Cruz, CA 95062
(831) 555-8485
DOB 7/19/1966
Dept: Marketing and Sales
Job Title: Sales
Start Date: 3/16/1999
SSN: 301-55-1918
Marital Status: S
Pay Status: H
Allowances: 0
Pay Rate: $17.25
Tax Bracket: S3

- Employee No 1005
  Juan X Santiago
  6746 Mission Blvd
  Santa Cruz, CA 95062
  (831) 555-7864
  DOB 6/17/1960
  Dept: Production
  Job Title: Production
  Start Date: 5/23/2001
  SSN: 600-55-5533
  Marital Status: M
  Pay Status: H
  Allowances: 2
  Pay Rate: $17.00
  Tax Bracket: S3

- Employee No 1006
  Charlie Murray
  2771 Dos Perros Drive
  Ben Lomand, CA 94583
  (831) 555-7488
  DOB 5/27/1973
  Dept: Production
  Job Title: Production Supervisor
  Start Date: 7/13/2001
  SSN: 734-79-6289
  Marital Status: S
  Pay Status: S
  Allowances: 0
  Pay Rate: $3,250.00
  Tax Bracket: S4

- Employee No 1007
  David M Jerusalem
  7364 Labrador Lane
  Scotts Valley, CA 95067
  (831) 555-9764
  DOB 4/14/1987
  Dept: Production
  Job Title: Production
  Start Date: 3/16/2000
  SSN: 601-74-5936
  Marital Status: S
  Pay Status: H
  Allowances: 0
  Pay Rate: $16.75
  Tax Bracket: S3

- Employee No 1008
  Theresa S Chung
  3819 Lazy Lane

Santa Cruz, CA 95062
(831) 555-7469
DOB 5/1/1989
Dept: Production
Job Title: Production
Start Date: 6/25/2011
SSN: 587-85-8474
Marital Status: S
Pay Status: H
Allowances: 0
Pay Rate: $16.00
Tax Bracket: S3

- Employee No 1009
Miguel C Santana
7227 Via de la Siesta
Santa Cruz, CA 95062
(831) 555-0847
DOB 8/31/1970
Dept: Accounting
Job Title: Controller
Start Date: 3/27/2002
SSN: 692-76-7384
Marital Status: M
Pay Status: S
Allowances: 1
Pay Rate: $3,250.00
Tax Bracket: M3

- Employee No 1010
Ned Walker
928 Enterprise Drive
Apt. 2A
Santa Cruz, CA 95062
(831) 555-9442
DOB 12/28/1980
Dept: Marketing and Sales
Job Title: Sales
Start Date: 12/13/2002
SSN: 643-67-5837
Marital Status: S
Pay Status: H
Allowances: 0
Pay Rate: $16.75
Tax Bracket: S3

- Employee No 1011
Edward E Israel
9766 Labrador Lane

Scotts Valley, CA 95067
(831) 555-9536
DOB 3/16/1989
Dept: Accounting
Job Title: Accounting clerk
Start Date: 11/21/2007
SSN: 501-38-9574
Marital Status: S
Pay Status: H
Allowances: 0
Pay Rate: $16.50
Tax Bracket: S3

- Employee No 1012
Brenda T Chan
9462 Monterey Lane
Scotts Valley, CA 95067
(831) 555-7316
DOB 2/9/1971
Dept: Marketing and Sales
Job Title: Sales
Start Date: 10/13/2010
SSN: 845-63-6956
Marital Status: S
Pay Status: H
Allowances: 0
Pay Rate: $16.50
Tax Bracket: S3

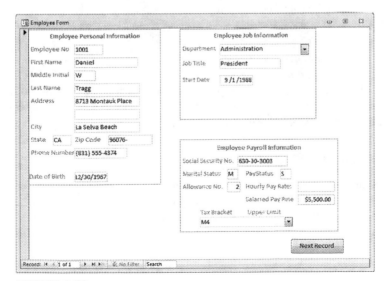

FIGURE 6-29

Tracking Time Worked

In order to calculate payroll, it is necessary to track the hours worked for hourly employees. The **Hours Worked Table** and **Hours Worked Form** have been created for this purpose. Since we have some employees who are production employees and some who are non-production employees, this table and form can be considered part of the Conversion Process. Therefore, we have not detailed the construction of these objects in this chapter. Some points are worth noting, however.

Now that we have created the **Employee Table** and **Employee Form**, we can populate the **Hours Worked Table**. Note that we only need to input data for hourly employees into this form. Open the **Hours Worked Form** and input the following data for the pay period ended 10/31/2012:

- Employee No 1004
  88 hours Regular Time
  1.2 hours Overtime
- Employee No 1005
  88 hours Regular Time
  2.7 hours Overtime
- Employee No 1007
  88 hours Regular Time
  0.3 hours Overtime
- Employee No 1008
  88 hours Regular Time
  0 hours Overtime
- Employee No 1010
  88 hours Regular Time
  0.1 hours Overtime
- Employee No 1011
  88 hours Regular Time
  0 hours Overtime
- Employee No 1012
  88 hours Regular Time
  0.4 hours Overtime

In addition, we have not yet created any relationships between any of the Human Resource Business Process tables yet. Click on **Database Tools** and create the necessary relationships between these tables at this time.

The Gross Pay Query

Now that we have employees, payroll data, and hours worked data, we can calculate the payroll. Arriving at net pay is a complex, multi-step process and requires the use of queries. We begin with the calculation of gross pay. The calculation for salaried employees and the calculation for hourly employees is slightly different. Therefore, we need to perform two different queries for gross pay and then merge the two queries together. To do this, we need to be sure that the two queries have matching fields and the same number of columns.

1. Click on the **Create** tab and double-click on **Query Design** icon.

2. From the **Show Table** window, click on the **Employee Table**, hold the **Ctrl** key down, and click on the **Hours Worked Table**. Click **Add** and then click **Close**.

3. Drag the **EmployeeNo** field from the **Hours Worked Table** into the first column of the design grid. Drag the **PPEnded**, **RegularTimeHours**, and **OvertimeHours** from the **Hours Worked Table** into the next columns of the design grid. Drag **HPayRate** from the **Employee Table** to the next column.

4. Click on the Field property in the sixth column of the design grid and click on the **Builder** Builder icon under the **Design** tab. Type **HRegularPay: [HPayRate]* [RegularTimeHours]** in the upper portion of the Expression Builder window (Figure 6-30). Click **OK**.

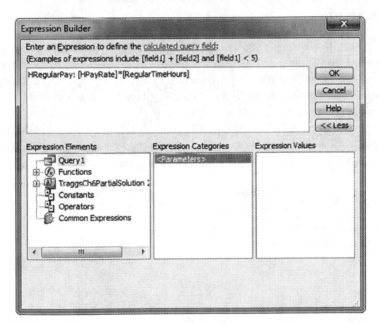

FIGURE 6-30

5. Click on the Field property in the seventh column of the design grid and click on the **Builder** Builder icon again. Type **HOvertimePay: 1.5* [HPayRate]* [OvertimeHours]** in the upper portion of the Expression Builder window (Figure 6-31). Click **OK**.

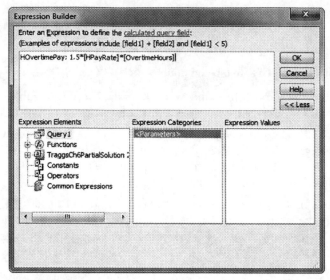

FIGURE 6-31

6. Before we can calculate the gross pay field, we need to create a field that will hold the place for the gross pay for salaried employees. Click on the **Field** property in the eighth column of the design grid. Type **Salary: 0** in the Field property. This results in creating a column with the field name "Salary" that is a place holder in this query so that we can join the salaried gross pay data later.

7. Click on the Field property in the ninth column of the design grid and click on the **Builder** ⚒ Builder icon once more. Type **GrossPay: [HRegularPay] + [HOvertimePay] + [Salary]** in the upper portion of the Expression Builder window (Figure 6-32). Click **OK**.

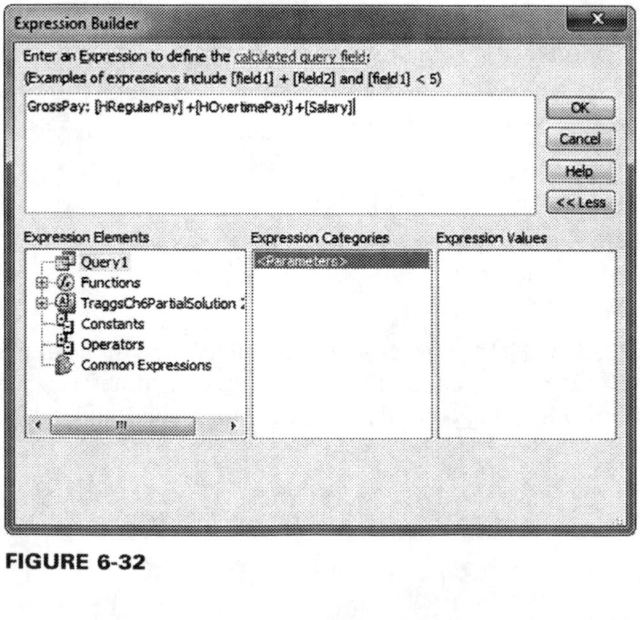

FIGURE 6-32

8. Click on the **Run** ⟋ Run icon. Close and save the query as **Gross Pay Hourly Query**.

9. Now we will create a query for the salaried employees. Click on **Query Design** under the **Create** tab again. Click on **Employee Table**. This is the only table we will need for salaried employees. Click on **Add** and **Close**.

10. Remember that we must eventually join this query with the query we just created for the hourly employees and, therefore, we must match the columns we created for this query. Open the **Gross Pay Hourly Query** and count the number of columns in that query. We see that, in addition to **EmployeeNo**, we had six fields that related to hourly employees. We then entered a field as a place holder for salaried employees. Finally, we calculated gross pay. Close the **Gross Pay Hourly Query**.

11. We know that we will want **EmployeeNo** in the first field for the salaried employees query. Drag that field from the **Employee Table** first field in the design grid.

12. In the next six Field properties, type a **0**. These columns will now act as place holders, just as the Salary column did in the **Gross Pay Hourly Query**.

13. Drag the **SPayRate** field from the **Employee Table** into the eighth column of the design grid. Click on the Criteria property and type **>0**. This will result in listing only those employees whose **SPayRate** are greater than zero or, in other words, only salaried employees.

14. Click on the Field property in the ninth column of the design grid and click on the **Builder** ⟋ Builder icon in the menu bar. Type **GrossPay: [SPayRate]*1** in the upper portion of the Expression Builder window (Figure 6-33). Click **OK**.

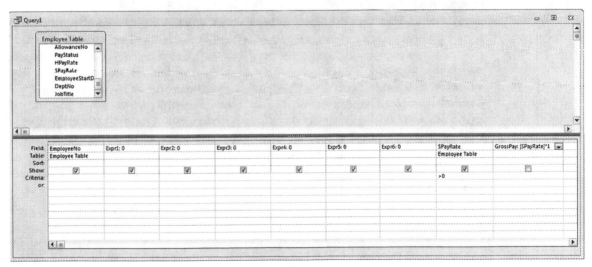

FIGURE 6-33

15. Click on the **Run** ⟋ Run icon. Close and save the query as **Gross Pay Salaried Query**.

16. We now have to join the two queries together. We will do this by creating a *union query*. A union query is a type of select query that combines fields from two or more tables or queries into one field in the query's results with any duplicate records removed. Click on **Query Design** under the **Create** section once more. Close the **Show table** window.

17. Click on **Union Query** ⚭ Union icon under the **Design** tab.

18. In the design screen for the union query (Figure 6-34), type the following SQL statement:

> **Select * from [Gross Pay Hourly Query]**
>
> **UNION Select * from [Gross Pay Salaried Query];**

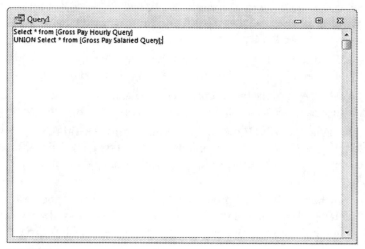

```
Query1
Select * from [Gross Pay Hourly Query]
UNION Select * from [Gross Pay Salaried Query];
```

FIGURE 6-34

19. Close and save the union query as **Gross Pay Union Query**.

We are now ready to calculate net pay. There are many deductions that can go into the calculation of net pay. We will simplify the calculation by limiting the deductions to payroll taxes, specifically Federal withholding tax (which we will abbreviate as FIT), FICA (Federal Insurance Corporation Act Tax for Social Security) and Medicare tax. We will ignore State withholding and other deductions such as medical insurance, retirement, etc.

20. Click on **Query Design** under the **Create** tab again. Click on the **Queries** tab in the **Show Table** window and click on the **Gross Pay Union Query**. Click **Add**. Click on the **Tables** tab. Click on the **Employee Table**, the **Withholding Table**, and the **Allowance Table**. Click **Close**.

21. Drag the **EmployeeNo** from the **Gross Pay Union Query** into the first Field property. Click on the Sort property and click on Ascending.

22. Drag **PPEnded** and **GrossPay** from **Gross Pay Union Query** into the second and third Field properties.

23. Drag **TaxRate**, **FWT** and **UpperLimit** from **Withholding Table** into the fourth, fifth, and sixth Field properties.

24. Drag **AllowanceAmount** from **Allowance Table** into seventh Field property.

The following steps relate to the calculation of payroll taxes. These calculations are relatively complex but they serve two important purposes. First, we have not yet learned about complex calculations in a database and they will allow us to practice them. Second, taxation is an important part of the study of accounting. The study of accounting information systems requires a solid understanding of the different aspects of accounting. It is important to keep in mind that *"accounting"* is the first word in AIS!

25. Click on the **Field** property in the eighth column of the design grid and click on the **Builder** 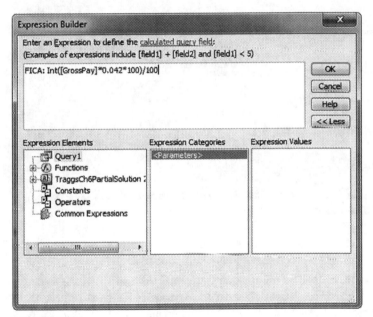 icon under the **Design** tab. Type **FICA: Int([GrossPay]* 0.042*100)/100** in the upper portion of the Expression Builder window (Figure 6-35). (Note that the authors are using the 4.2% FICA tax rate in effect in 2011 and projected to be continued through 2012 at this writing.) The **Int** function removes the fractional part of the number and returns the resulting integer value. This is necessary for our calculation here because we are multiplying **GrossPay** (a dollar amount) by a percentage and we want our result to be in dollars and cents. Click **OK** and click out of the **FICA** field.

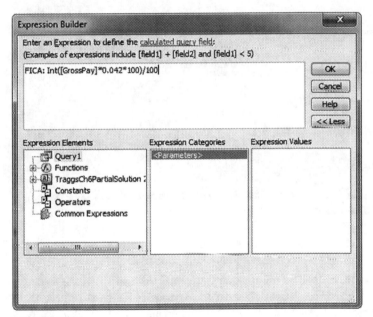

FIGURE 6-35

26. Right-click on the **FICA** field and click on **Properties**. Click on **Format** and using the pull-down menu, change the **Format** to **Currency**.

27. Click on the Field property in the ninth column of the design grid and click on the **Builder** Builder icon once more. Type **Medicare: Int([GrossPay]*0.0145*100)/100** in the upper portion of the Expression Builder window. Click **OK** and click out of the **Medicare** field. Format the **Medicare** field for **Currency** also.

28. Click on the Field property in the tenth column of the design grid and click on the **Builder** Builder icon again. Type **FIT: (([GrossPay]-** in the upper portion of the Expression Builder window. Open the Database in lower left portion of the window and click on **Tables**. Click on the **Allowance Table**. Double-click on **AllowanceAmount** in the middle of the lower portion of the Expression Builder window and click on the – (minus) symbol.

29. Click on the **Withholding Table** and double-click on **UpperLimit** in the middle of the lower portion of the Expression Builder window, and type)* .

30. Double-click on **TaxRate** in the middle of the lower portion of the Expression Builder window, type) + and double-click on **FWT** in the middle of the lower portion of the Expression Builder window (Figure 6-36). Click **OK**.

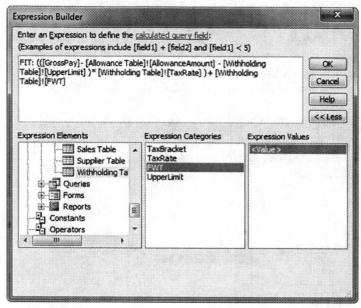

FIGURE 6-36

31. Click in the eleventh column of the design grid and type **NetPay: [GrossPay]-[FIT]-[FICA]-[Medicare]** in the Field property.

32. Before we run the query, we need to be sure that the formatting of the remaining fields is correct. Right-click on the **GrossPay** field and click on Properties. Click on **Format** and using the pull-down menu, change the Format to Currency. Do the same for the **FIT** and **NetPay** fields.

33. Click on the Run ! icon. Close and save the query as **Net Pay Query**.

KEY TERMS

Union query

QUESTIONS AND PROBLEMS FOR REVIEW

MULTIPLE-CHOICE QUESTIONS

6.1 Tables in the human resource business process can

(a) store reference data for use in calculating gross pay and payroll tax.

(b) link employees and departments.

(c) store payroll registers.

(d) contain only one primary key.

(e) All of the above.

6.2 The primary key for the Hours Worked Table should be:

(a) the employee number.

(b) the department number.

(c) the employee number and the pay period.

(d) the employee number and the department number.

(e) None of the above.

6.3 The purpose of a union query is to

(a) add records from the database table that you are using to another database table.

(b) combine fields from two or more tables or queries into one field in the query's results with any duplicate records removed.

(c) retrieve information that you want from one or more tables in a database and present the information that you retrieved in a format that you desire.

(d) None of the above.

PROBLEMS

6.1 Dan Tragg has asked you to create a Payroll Register as of September 30, 2006.

6.2 Tragg's has also decided to print their Payroll checks and related earnings statements for their employees each period. Design this report. (Note: Create it so that it is one report that would result in the Payroll check being torn off the bottom for deposit in the bank.)

INDEX